S0-BZR-207

Visit Resurgence Publishing online at theResurgence.com.

Resurgence Publishing, Inc., the Resurgence "R," and Resurgence wordmark are registered trademarks of Resurgence.

Acts Study Guide: Chapters 6–11

Cover design: Mars Hill Creative

ISBN-10: 1-938805-24-0
ISBN-13: 978-1-938805-24-0

Printed in the United States of America

20   19   18   17   16   15   14
7   6   5   4   3   2   1

CONTENTS

INTRODUCTION

"If this plan or this undertaking is of man, it will fail; but if it is of
God, you will not be able to overthrow them."—Acts 5:38–39

Just before he ascended into heaven, the resurrected Jesus left his followers with a promise: "You will receive power" (Acts 1:8). The book of Acts
records the true story of this power unleashed among them through the
Holy Spirit.

The Holy Spirit is the third member of the Trinity, equal to God the
Father and God the Son, Jesus. God the Spirit is the main character in the
book of Acts and the primary agent of history to this day. He is active in the
world and alive in the hearts of all who trust in Jesus, providing them wisdom,
courage, hope, and peace that transcends circumstances.

In the section of Acts that you will study in this book, we see a variety of
ways in which the Holy Spirit accomplishes the will of God. From miraculous
displays of supernatural glory (e.g., 9:17–18, 40–42) to tragic events redeemed
for good (e.g., 8:4–8), nothing can stop the power of God and the mission he
seeks to fulfill.

Before Christianity was the world's largest religion, it was a small movement birthed out of traditional Judaism. As we learn in Acts, however, it did not
stay small for long. Jesus' initial followers faithfully proclaimed the good news
of salvation, and the Holy Spirit surged to fill new people from different races,
cultures, and nations, far exceeding any human expectation.

The book of Acts describes a unique moment in history, but not an iso-
lated moment. The same Holy Spirit that changed the world two thousand
years ago is still changing it today. The same mission that took salvation from
Jerusalem to Asia, Africa, Europe, and beyond oceans is still our mission today.

The same power that carried the church of God through insurmountable obstacles is still a source of strength and joy for us today.

Jesus' power through the Holy Spirit has, does, and will prevail over all other powers. This *is* of God—just as Christianity's early opponents suspected (5:38–39). Nothing could stop it in the first century, and nothing can stop it in the twenty-first century.

May the Holy Spirit bless you with great confidence in him as you study his work and then do the acts he is leading you to do for the glory of Jesus, the good of his church, the joy of your heart, and the salvation of others.

—**Pastor Mark Driscoll**

COMPONENTS OF THIS STUDY GUIDE

This study guide is the result of a collaborative effort between Mars Hill Church staff, Docent Research Group, and faithful volunteers.

1. Daily Devotions
2. Small Group Study Guide
3. Inductive Study Guide

The Daily Devotions were written in order to facilitate dinnertime conversation with your family. These reflections are geared toward a younger audience but are written in a way that will be challenging to all. Five devotions are provided for each week's Scripture passage, and you're encouraged to use these in whatever way best fits the weekly rhythms of your family.

The Small Group Study is intended for small group Bible studies. Many churches encourage these types of midweek studies, but each share the same goal—that the people of God gather together in community to study the Word, encourage one another, pray, and get equipped for the mission of making the gospel of Jesus known to one another, their families, and their communities.

The Group Inductive Study approach encourages digging deep into Scripture and employs an in-depth reading technique designed for a discussion-based setting. An inductive study asks the questions, "What does the Bible say, and what does it mean?" "What do we observe, and how should we interpret it in light of the whole truth of the Bible?" This portion of the study guide focuses on delving deep into the text in a collaborative environment and is a great complement to the Daily Devotions and Small Group Study material.

For additional resources on how to use these studies, please refer to the Appendix for Leaders.

DAILY DEVOTIONS

WEEK 1

Acts 6:1–7

DAY 1

God's care for the weak

> [6:1] Now in these days when the disciples were increasing in number, a complaint by the Hellenists arose against the Hebrews because their widows were being neglected in the daily distribution. [2] And the twelve summoned the full number of the disciples and said, "It is not right that we should give up preaching the word of God to serve tables."

Who do you think are the most needy people in our society? The homeless? The mentally ill? Certainly, people who fall into those categories are very needy, but the Bible focuses on one particular disadvantaged group: widows.

In first-century Palestine, women were not allowed to work outside the home, so they relied on their husbands to provide for them financially. But if their husbands were deceased, they had no way of taking care of themselves. There was no welfare net for the poor. So the responsibility to care for widows fell on the church.

But this task was often thwarted by factions and cliques, denying widows their basic necessities. You can understand how this would be a problem, right?

Something had to change. It was important that the church solve this problem because there was to be no favoritism of one group over another, period. Jesus died for all people and wants no division.

Read James 1:27

- What is God's heart for the weak, needy, and marginalized?
- How does your church or small group contribute to the needs of these groups?

DAILY DEVOTIONS

- How can we remember to not show favoritism to certain groups of people in our church?

Prayer

Father, thank you that you have brought all types of people into your community. We want to remember that you loved us even when we were so different from you—you died for us while we were still sinners. May this truth revolutionize how we view those who are different from us. In Jesus' name we pray. Amen.

DAY 2

The primacy of the Word and prayer

[6:1] Now in these days when the disciples were increasing in number, a complaint by the Hellenists arose against the Hebrews because their widows were being neglected in the daily distribution. [2] And the twelve summoned the full number of the disciples and said, "It is not right that we should give up preaching the word of God to serve tables."

Do you know what it means to "delegate"?

It means to entrust to another person a job for which you are ultimately responsible.

As was discussed yesterday, the job of caring for widows at that time fell on the church, and the apostles were ultimately responsible. But they didn't have the power to be everywhere all the time and therefore needed help to ensure that the whole community was healthy.

Because few could do the work of an apostle—e.g., preach and pray—they delegated to "deacons," members called to fulfill the church's varied needs.

Leaders of the church need to specialize in their main duties and delegate other tasks in order to cultivate God's church.

Read 2 Timothy 4:1–2

- What is the command in this text from Paul to Timothy?
- What would happen if our leaders didn't devote themselves to preaching and prayer?

Prayer

Father, thank you that you have given different gifts of service to various kinds of people in your church. May your church operate like a healthy body, with everyone using the gifts you've given them. May we be a light to the world in the way we love and serve one another. Help our leaders, especially, to be faithful in teaching and prayer. In Jesus' name we pray. Amen.

DAY 3

Faithful servants

[6:3] "Therefore, brothers, pick out from among you seven men of good repute, full of the Spirit and of wisdom, whom we will appoint to this duty. [4] But we will devote ourselves to prayer and to the ministry of the word." [5] And what they said pleased the whole gathering, and they chose Stephen, a man full of faith and of the Holy Spirit, and Philip, and Prochorus, and Nicanor, and Timon, and Parmenas, and Nicolaus, a proselyte of Antioch. [6] These they set before the apostles, and they prayed and laid their hands on them.

If you were responsible for executing a very important task and had to delegate, what kind of person would you want to delegate to? Someone who had a track record of lying? Someone who tended to steal? Someone who always ran their mouth and never listened to anyone else?

Probably not. You would want to delegate to someone who was trustworthy, had good character, and was willing and able to do the task at hand.

That's exactly what the early church leaders did when they realized there were tangible needs arising that they themselves couldn't fulfill. So they found men "of good repute, full of the Spirit and of wisdom" and appointed them to care for the widows in their community.

Character matters. These men had to have a good reputation, the fullness of the Spirit as evidenced by its fruits, and wisdom—three characteristics you should look for in someone when delegating a task.

Read 1 Timothy 3:8–13

- Why is having a good reputation, the Spirit, and wisdom so important for deacons?
- What other characteristics are important for deacons?
- Could you see yourself as a deacon?

Prayer

Father, thank you that you have given faithful servants to the church. Help us all to have a good reputation, show the fruits of the Spirit, and be wise. In Jesus' name we pray. Amen.

DAY 4

Rapid increase

[6:7] And the word of God continued to increase, and the number of the disciples multiplied greatly in Jerusalem, and a great many of the priests became obedient to the faith.

One of the things we have learned in these verses is that God desires his church to be healthy, because he loves the church and the people he has called the church to reach.

Right after dealing with the neglect of the widows, the text reports that the word of God increased mightily and many more people decided to follow Jesus and were added to the church.

The text uses the word "multiply." How is "multiply" different from "add"? If you know a little bit about math, you know that you can arrive at a much bigger number more quickly by multiplying than by adding. For example, if you wanted to arrive at twenty-five, you could do that by calculating "5 x 5." Compare that to adding: "5 + 5 + 5 + 5 + 5." It's a bit longer and takes more work. See the difference?

When the Bible speaks about multiplication in this verse, it implies speed of growth. As the church was faithful to what God had called them to, God added to their numbers greatly.

Read Acts 2:42–47

- What does a healthy church look like according to these verses?
- How can you help your church become more healthy?
- How have you seen God add to your numbers at church?

Prayer

Father, thank you for multiplying the first church. We would not be here as a church if they had died out. We are standing on the shoulders of their faithfulness. May we make good disciples so that there can be future generations of healthy churches. In Jesus' name we pray. Amen.

DAY 5

Leaders convert

> [6:7] And the word of God continued to increase, and the number of the disciples multiplied greatly in Jerusalem, and a great many of the priests became obedient to the faith.

What kind of unbelieving person do you think is the least likely to convert to Christianity? This can be a misleading question—God can convert anyone he wants and, in fact, he has saved people from all walks of life all throughout history. But just for the sake of discussion, who do you think would be the least likely to convert?

During the first century, it might have been the Jewish priests, ironically enough. They were the ones who showed the greatest opposition to Jesus and his followers in the early days of his ministry and the church. To have a "great many" of them convert and follow Jesus later must have been quite a shake-up in Jerusalem.

When God saves those you think would be the last people to repent and believe, we know that it is truly God's work. God did it in the early church, and he still does it today!

Read 2 Corinthians 4:7–12

- How does God show up in unexpected places in these verses?
- Who in your life seems unlikely to convert that you need to pray for?
- Who do you know that has been converted in a dramatic way?

Prayer

Father, thank you that you can save anyone. We stand in awe of the fact that you would use weak vessels like us to save those who are perishing. May we continue to see the "unexpected" come into your kingdom. We know that nobody deserves to be saved and that anytime someone is, it's by your grace. Thank you, Father. In Jesus' name we pray. Amen.

WEEK 2

Acts 6:8–8:3

DAY 1

Stephen, filled by the Spirit, persecuted by men

[6:8] And Stephen, full of grace and power, was doing great wonders and signs among the people. [9] Then some of those who belonged to the synagogue of the Freedmen (as it was called), and of the Cyrenians, and of the Alexandrians, and of those from Cilicia and Asia, rose up and disputed with Stephen. [10] But they could not withstand the wisdom and the Spirit with which he was speaking. [11] Then they secretly instigated men who said, "We have heard him speak blasphemous words against Moses and God." [12] And they stirred up the people and the elders and the scribes, and they came upon him and seized him and brought him before the council, [13] and they set up false witnesses who said, "This man never ceases to speak words against this holy place and the law, [14] for we have heard him say that this Jesus of Nazareth will destroy this place and will change the customs that Moses delivered to us." [15] And gazing at him, all who sat in the council saw that his face was like the face of an angel.

Have you ever competed in a game against an opponent who was extremely competitive? So competitive, in fact, that they were willing to cheat to beat you? If so, you know how challenging and frustrating it can be. If both players are not playing by the same rules, the one attempting to be honest will almost always lose.

We find a similar situation in today's text. Stephen was a man who was filled with the Spirit of God, preaching the Good News to his community fearlessly. Those who hated his message knew they couldn't defeat his preaching

17

through normal means, so they resorted to more sinister tactics. In short, they cheated: they discredited his reputation and flat out lied about him.

Sadly, there are people who hate God's message, and if they can't defeat it, they'll do whatever they can to discredit the messenger. This shouldn't cause us to fear because God will be with us no matter what. But we should expect to face such opposition if we are being faithful like Stephen.

Read 2 Timothy 3:12–14

- Why do you think this verse says that living in godliness will lead to persecution?
- Have you ever been persecuted for your faith? If not, how do you think you'd handle it?

Prayer

Father, help us to persevere when our faith is tested through persecution. We need your help to stand strong and bear witness to the fact that our greatest hope is not in the world but in you. In Jesus' name we pray. Amen.

DAY 2

Abraham, the father of faith

[7:1] And the high priest said, "Are these things so?" [2] And Stephen said:

"Brothers and fathers, hear me. The God of glory appeared to our father Abraham when he was in Mesopotamia, before he lived in Haran, [3] and said to him, 'Go out from your land and from your kindred and go into the land that I will show you.' [4] Then he went out from the land of the Chaldeans and lived in Haran. And after his father died, God removed him from there into this land in which you are now living. [5] Yet he gave him no inheritance in it, not even a foot's length, but promised to give it to him as a possession and to his offspring after him, though he had no child. [6] And God spoke to this effect—that his offspring would be sojourners in a land belonging to others, who would enslave them and afflict them four hundred years. [7] 'But I will judge the nation that they serve,' said God, 'and after that they shall come out and worship me in this place.' [8] And he gave him the covenant of circumcision. And so Abraham became the father of Isaac, and circumcised him on the eighth day, and Isaac became the father of Jacob, and Jacob of the twelve patriarchs.

Stephen faced the accusations made against him by the religious leaders, the same leaders who killed Jesus. He appealed to them through what they all knew, their shared history as the Jewish people, explaining how faith in the Old Testament promises of God pointed to Jesus.

He started by recounting the promises God had made to Abraham—to provide offspring, even though his wife was too old to have children; to give him a land, even though he couldn't comprehend where that would be; and to be his faithful protector. These promises were confirmed by circumcision, a physical sign of covenant between them.

Stephen declared that all of God's promises to Abraham had come to pass in Jesus. As we will see in the coming days, Stephen demonstrated how Jesus was the promised Messiah, and the religious leaders missed it—they were blinded by their hatred for him.

Read Deuteronomy 7:9

- What does this verse tell us about the character of God?
- How have God's promises come true in your life?

Prayer

Father, thank you that we can trust your Word. Guard us from the Evil One, whose sole mission is to cause us to hate you and reject your Word. May we always have soft hearts, not hard hearts of unbelief. Help us. We need help. In Jesus' name we pray. Amen.

DAY 3

A deliverer for God's people

[7:9] "And the patriarchs, jealous of Joseph, sold him into Egypt; but God was with him [10] and rescued him out of all his afflictions and gave him favor and wisdom before Pharaoh, king of Egypt, who made him ruler over Egypt and over all his household. [11] Now there came a famine throughout all Egypt and Canaan, and great affliction, and our fathers could find no food. [12] But when Jacob heard that there was grain in Egypt, he sent out our fathers on their first visit. [13] And on the second visit Joseph made himself known to his brothers, and Joseph's family became known to Pharaoh. [14] And Joseph sent and summoned Jacob his father and all his kindred, seventy-five persons in all. [15] And Jacob went down into Egypt, and he died, he and our fathers, [16] and they were carried back to Shechem and laid in the tomb that Abraham had bought for a sum of silver from the sons of Hamor in Shechem.

[17] "But as the time of the promise drew near, which God had granted to Abraham, the people increased and multiplied in Egypt [18] until there arose over Egypt another king who did not know Joseph. [19] He dealt shrewdly with our race and forced our fathers to expose their infants, so that they would not be kept alive. [20] At this time Moses was born; and he was beautiful in God's sight. And he was brought up for three months in his father's house, [21] and when he was exposed, Pharaoh's daughter adopted him and brought him up as her own son. [22] And Moses was instructed in all the wisdom of the Egyptians, and he was mighty in his words and deeds."

God always keeps his promises. But sometimes these promises come to pass through suffering. This truth is most clear in the life of Jesus but also appears in the lives of other prominent biblical figures, like Abraham and Moses.

Stephen summarizes the events of what took place after Abraham: Abraham's kids, grandkids, and great grandkids moved to Egypt. There, generation after generation arose, and God's people grew quite large over the course of a few centuries. After many years had passed, there rose to power a pharaoh who despised these descendants of Abraham, enslaving them for many years.

God finally decided to put an end to their oppression and raise up for them a leader named Moses, who nearly died but God spared through someone from pharaoh's own household. This Moses would be like a son to the pharaoh until God would call him out from pharaoh's house to lead his people out of slavery. Moses would be a forerunner of our true deliverer, Jesus, who would rescue the whole world from slavery to sin.

God's promises continued to march on. Stephen wanted these people to see this and believe.

Read Psalm 18:2

- How does this psalm align with what Stephen shared?
- How have you seen God's deliverance?

Prayer
Father, thank you that you promise to deliver us and, in fact, you have delivered us from our bondage to sin and death. You conquered these things by the power of your resurrection. In Jesus' name we pray. Amen.

DAY 4

The rest of the story

Optional: Read Acts 7:23–53.

Stephen goes on to tell them the rest of the story in order to make his point: God's people, the nation of Israel, time and time again, rejected God's provision for them. They complained to Moses their deliverer, and rejected and killed the prophets that God raised up for them. What Stephen is saying is, "You're doing the same thing! You need to repent!"

Sadly, most people, when they hear the call to repentance, harden their hearts and close their ears.

Why do you think it is so hard to repent?

Repenting demonstrates that we are needy—we're not God. God is the only person in the universe who doesn't need to repent because he always does what is just and right. We don't. We are sinners. We need help. We need forgiveness. We need healing and atonement for our sin.

In this account, Stephen is pointing out their hypocrisy. They claim to be religious, but their actions tell a different story. They need to repent of their hypocrisy. The religious leaders hated Jesus for exactly the same reasons they hated Stephen: he accused them of failing to lead God's people.

One of the things that God hates the most is hypocrisy. He wants his people to follow him as he has declared, not as they see fit. But instead of repenting of their sin, they rejected God and his messenger.

Read Mark 1:15

- Why do you think Jesus said this when he began his ministry?
- Why does God love it when we repent?
- What things do you need to repent of?
- When we repent, what assurance do we have that God will forgive? (Read 1 John 1:8–10.)

Prayer

Father, help us to not be like Stephen's audience. We don't want to have stiff necks and hardened hearts. We want to be softhearted toward you. Help us to repent even when we don't want to face our sin and its consequences. Help us to love you more than our sin and our need to be right all the time. Thank you that Jesus promises to forgive our sin when we repent. In Jesus' name we pray. Amen.

DAY 5

Persecution, pain, and God's pleasure

[7:54] Now when they heard these things they were enraged, and they ground their teeth at him. [55] But he, full of the Holy Spirit, gazed into heaven and saw the glory of God, and Jesus standing at the right hand of God. [56] And he said, "Behold, I see the heavens opened, and the Son of Man standing at the right hand of God." [57] But they cried out with a loud voice and stopped their ears and rushed together at him. [58] Then they cast him out of the city and stoned him. And the witnesses laid down their garments at the feet of a young man named Saul. [59] And as they were stoning Stephen, he called out, "Lord Jesus, receive my spirit." [60] And falling to his knees he cried out with a loud voice, "Lord, do not hold this sin against them." And when he had said this, he fell asleep.

[8:1] And Saul approved of his execution. And there arose on that day a great persecution against the church in Jerusalem, and they were all scattered throughout the regions of Judea and Samaria, except the apostles. [2] Devout men buried Stephen and made great lamentation over him. [3] But Saul was ravaging the church, and entering house after house, he dragged off men and women and committed them to prison.

Telling the truth is always the right thing to do. That is what Stephen did. Unfortunately many people fail to love the truth and are more than willing to persecute those who tell the truth.

Have you ever had someone hate you because you told the truth? Maybe you saw someone doing something they shouldn't, and a teacher or parent asked you about it. You felt constrained to tell the truth, and as a result, that person got in trouble. Then the person who got in trouble was angry at you for telling on them. They didn't like being exposed. They should have repented of their sin, but instead they wanted to hide it. By you telling the truth about them, you made their situation more uncomfortable, and so they retaliated: They might have made fun of you. They might have laughed at you. Maybe they even tried to steal something from you.

All this and more happened to Stephen. They killed him by throwing stones at him. They unjustly killed him because he told the truth, and they hated his message because they hated the truth.

But notice how full of mercy Stephen was. Just like Jesus on the cross, Stephen prayed to God to forgive those who were persecuting him. When people are filled with the Spirit of God, they will be full of mercy, even for those who seek to harm them.

Read Ephesians 2:4–5

- How does God demonstrate his mercy in these two verses?
- Who in your life right now do you need to show mercy to?

Prayer

Father, thank you for showing us mercy while we were dead in our sins. May we show that same kind of mercy to those who hate the truth. Help us to endure with love when we tell the truth and people respond with hate. We need your Spirit to lead and guide us in these difficult situations. In Jesus' name we pray. Amen.

WEEK 3

Acts 8:4–25

DAY 1

Bad things turn into good things

> [8:4] Now those who were scattered went about preaching the word. [5] Philip went down to the city of Samaria and proclaimed to them the Christ. [6] And the crowds with one accord paid attention to what was being said by Philip when they heard him and saw the signs that he did. [7] For unclean spirits, crying out with a loud voice, came out of many who had them, and many who were paralyzed or lame were healed. [8] So there was much joy in that city.

Have you ever had something really bad happen, but after some time passed, it led to something good? Maybe you had to move away from your friends because your dad got a new job. But eventually, you made some other great friends. Sometimes really hard things lead to really good things.

That was the case with the church. The church was forced to spread out to other places because the persecution was severe in Jerusalem. But this allowed them to share their faith with all sorts of people who had never heard the good news of Jesus.

Oftentimes we can't see what God is doing when seemingly bad things happen to us. When the people of the early church were being severely persecuted after the martyrdom of Stephen, many of them certainly questioned God's plan, asking why God allowed him to be killed.

God had a plan for his kingdom to expand to the ends of the earth, and nothing could stop that. He even used Stephen's martyrdom to help carry out that plan.

Read Romans 8:28

- What is the promise of this verse?
- How should this verse be a comfort for us?
- How does this verse relate to today's text?

Prayer

Father, thank you for promising to never leave us or forsake us. Help us to trust you when we are called to endure things that are particularly challenging. Help us to believe that you have a plan even when it seems like you don't. We know that no matter what comes to pass, you promise to one day make all things right in the end. We hope and long for that day. In Jesus' name we pray. Amen.

DAY 2

Simon the magician

[8:9] But there was a man named Simon, who had previously practiced magic in the city and amazed the people of Samaria, saying that he himself was somebody great. [10] They all paid attention to him, from the least to the greatest, saying, "This man is the power of God that is called Great." [11] And they paid attention to him because for a long time he had amazed them with his magic. [12] But when they believed Philip as he preached good news about the kingdom of God and the name of Jesus Christ, they were baptized, both men and women. [13] Even Simon himself believed, and after being baptized he continued with Philip. And seeing signs and great miracles performed, he was amazed.

Sometimes very unlikely people come to faith in Jesus. Sometimes it's the last people that you would ever think would repent and trust Jesus who actually do! God is so good to show us that salvation is all of grace and not based on works. Sometimes the vilest of sinners awake to their need for a Savior.

We meet someone like this in today's text. Simon was a magician. We don't know for sure what that means. His abilities could have been supernatural and empowered by the devil, or it could simply have been tricks that he played on people. Either way, he was driven to win their marvel and honor.

God hates pride. Why do you think that is?

God hated the pride of Simon, and he hates the pride that can easily swell up in our hearts. Pride says to God, "I don't need you. I am good all on my own. I've got this, and if that changes, I'll let you know. But as of right now, I can manage my life all by myself."

Thankfully God's Spirit was more powerful than Simon's magic, and he drew Simon to himself. God can even save prideful people who think they don't need God. If God could save Simon, do you think there is anyone that God can't save?

This should give us great confidence in evangelism. We simply share the Good News and then pray for God to draw people to himself by his Spirit.

Read John 6:44

- Why is this verse a comfort for us when we share our faith like Philip?
- Who do you know appears to be the type of person who will not repent and trust Jesus? How could this verse inform how you pray for them?

Prayer

Father, thank you that you are not paralyzed by our prideful resistance. Thank you that we can trust you to do the work in people's hearts as we share the good news. May you save people like Simon. Please do it for Jesus' sake. In Jesus' name we pray. Amen.

DAY 3

The giving of the Holy Spirit

[8:14] Now when the apostles at Jerusalem heard that Samaria had received the word of God, they sent to them Peter and John, [15] who came down and prayed for them that they might receive the Holy Spirit, [16] for he had not yet fallen on any of them, but they had only been baptized in the name of the Lord Jesus. [17] Then they laid their hands on them and they received the Holy Spirit.

Sometimes we do special things for special reasons. If you have cancer, you might have to make frequent trips to the doctor. If you are an injured football player, you might have to work extra hard to get back on the field. If you have hurt someone with your words, you might have to make a special trip to meet with that person and apologize.

In today's text, Peter and John had to make a special trip to those who had recently become Christians, the Samaritans. Historically, the Samaritans were the archenemies of the Jewish people. Despite that, God intended the good news about Jesus to go to all people, not just the Jews.

What is interesting about this text is that it says that once they became Christians, they did not receive the Holy Spirit immediately but had to wait for Peter and John to come and lay their hands on them. Perhaps this was because there had been centuries-long hatred between these groups, and God might have wanted the leaders of this new church to go and physically lay hands on these converts as a gesture of full acceptance into the new Christian community.

All people are welcome. When the leaders of the church go and make this public declaration, it serves the church well.

Read Galatians 3:28

- What does this verse have to do with today's text?
- Why does God want disciples of Jesus from all different walks of life?
- How do you need to grow in loving all different types of people?

Prayer

Father, thank you that you have saved people from all different walks of life for your glory. You have created us all in your image and love all those you have made. Help us to love and serve all people regardless of who they are or where they come from. Thank you for pursuing us, Jews, Samaritans, and everyone else in the whole world by your Spirit. In Jesus' name we pray. Amen.

DAY 4

Writing checks to Jesus

[8:18] Now when Simon saw that the Spirit was given through the laying on of the apostles' hands, he offered them money, [19] saying, "Give me this power also, so that anyone on whom I lay my hands may receive the Holy Spirit." [20] But Peter said to him, "May your silver perish with you, because you thought you could obtain the gift of God with money!"

Even after we meet Jesus and receive salvation, our sin doesn't disappear. We have to be sanctified, or grow in holiness. Through sanctification, we learn to repent of sin and become more like Jesus.

Simon, whom we read about in this text, had also just begun his own process of sanctification. We learned a couple days ago that prior to becoming Christian, he was a very popular magician, who loved showing off his skills to the Samaritans. He had special influence over them, and he probably liked it.

Once he saw that Peter and John had a unique power from God for their special place in history, he wanted a share in this power, too. He went so far as to offer money to Peter and John in order to get it.

Isn't it sad to think you could buy what only God can give? God owns everything and doesn't need our cash.

Simon had a lot to learn about what it meant to be Christian. But we all do, right? Thankfully God is patient and kind. He loves it when we repent and turn to him in the midst of our failures. Isn't it great to know that the God we serve loves to help us?

Read John 17:17

- According to this verse, how do we get sanctified?
- In what ways do you believe you need to grow?
- Take some time to confess sin and areas you need to grow, and pray that God would do this in our lives by his Spirit.

Prayer

Father, thank you that you promise to work in and through us to make us more and more like Jesus. May we pursue you and your Word so that we can grow. We know that we'd starve without it. Thank you giving us your Word and your Spirit. In Jesus' name we pray. Amen.

DAY 5

Rebuke and repentance

[8:21] "You have neither part nor lot in this matter, for your heart is not right before God. [22] Repent, therefore, of this wickedness of yours, and pray to the Lord that, if possible, the intent of your heart may be forgiven you. [23] For I see that you are in the gall of bitterness and in the bond of iniquity." [24] And Simon answered, "Pray for me to the Lord, that nothing of what you have said may come upon me."

Have you ever had someone say a hard, challenging word to you that stung, but after the sting wore off, you could see clearly that it was exactly what you needed to hear?

Oftentimes, when we are knee-deep in sin, it's hard for us to see our way out. We need someone to wake us up. For some people, it takes the equivalent of a two-by-four to the head—a strong, direct word to show us the depth of our sin. Without it, we simply wouldn't respond.

Simon was a guy like that. He was knee-deep in his own sin of selfishness, trying to buy God's gifts with money. This was a grievous error. He needed a strong word to call him to repentance, and that's exactly what Peter did. Fortunately, Simon was awakened to his need for forgiveness. He sought the help of others and asked for prayer. This displayed dependence on others and on God, which God loves to honor.

When we are corrected by parents, teachers, pastors, or friends, we show true wisdom when we ask for help and pursue forgiveness. God loves it when we respond to our sin this way. May it be so of us!

Read 1 John 1:8–10

- What is the promise in this verse for those who repent?
- What do we learn about God's character in these verses?
- How have you tended to respond to rebuke?

Prayer

Father, our hearts are often prone to sin. Help us to love you more than we love sin. Help us to be quick to repent like Simon when we are in sin. Help us to listen well to others that love us and want to see us grow in holiness. We need help. That is clear. Help us by your Word, your people, and your Spirit for the sake of your glory and our growth in you. In Jesus' name we pray. Amen.

WEEK 4

Acts 8:26–40

DAY 1

A gospel for all nations

> [8:26] Now an angel of the Lord said to Philip, "Rise and go toward the south to the road that goes down from Jerusalem to Gaza." This is a desert place. [27] And he rose and went. And there was an Ethiopian, a eunuch, a court official of Candace, queen of the Ethiopians, who was in charge of all her treasure. He had come to Jerusalem to worship [28] and was returning, seated in his chariot, and he was reading the prophet Isaiah.

Have you ever felt left out? Perhaps you were that last one to know something or the last to be chosen for a team. Were you the one that didn't get the memo?

No one likes to be left out. It hurts. You know why? Because we were created for community. God exists as a community. He is Father, Son, and Holy Spirit, and when he created us to be like him (in his image), we too were created for community. This is one huge reason why we don't like to be left out.

Thankfully, God's community leaves no one out. His community is one where everyone is invited and everyone is included. Everyone is free to repent of sin and come to Jesus for forgiveness and life.

We see this clearly in the text. The book of Acts started with Jesus telling his first followers that they would be his witnesses of the gospel, not to just other Jewish people but to all nations.

That is exactly what we see happening in this verse. The gospel had not yet reached the nation of Ethiopia, and God wanted them to be able to repent and believe as well. So the Spirit of God compelled Philip to go and share with this man from Ethiopia.

In God's kingdom, no one is excluded. All men and women are welcome. God desires all nations to come and experience the joy of life in him.

Read Revelation 7:9–10

- At the consummation of all things, what do we see?
- How is your church reaching out to other nations?
- How can you make sure that continues to happen? How can you bless that effort?

Prayer

Father, thank you that you have excluded no one from your kingdom. You welcome all those who repent of their sin and believe the gospel. May we be like Philip—sensitive to your Spirit and your desire for all to come to know you. Through our giving, praying, and going, may your blessing be felt by all nations! In Jesus' name we pray. Amen.

DAY 2

The great combination

[8:26] Now an angel of the Lord said to Philip, "Rise and go toward the south to the road that goes down from Jerusalem to Gaza." This is a desert place. [27] And he rose and went. And there was an Ethiopian, a eunuch, a court official of Candace, queen of the Ethiopians, who was in charge of all her treasure. He had come to Jerusalem to worship [28] and was returning, seated in his chariot, and he was reading the prophet Isaiah.

There are many famous combinations that we enjoy in our world: Peanut butter and jelly. Steak and potatoes. Movies and music. (Could you imagine a movie without good music?) Hot chocolate and cold winter days. Campfires and roasted marshmallows. Christmas trees and presents. Certain things just make the perfect combination.

Can you think of some other examples?

God has a favorite combination as well. In fact, he has many of them. A couple of examples would be repentance and faith, or marriage between a man and a woman. But one combination we see clearly in today's text is the combination of Word and Spirit. In the book of Acts, God's gospel always flows out of the mouths of those who are filled with his Spirit. God loves to see his message go forth in the power of the Spirit of God.

Consider how anyone gets saved. We hear the gospel, God draws us to himself through the power of the Spirit (John 6:44), and we repent and believe. That is how anyone becomes a Christian. The gospel and the work of God's Spirit always go hand in hand.

In today's text, Philip is compelled by the Spirit to go and approach a foreigner who happens to be reading God's Word. The Spirit was compelling Philip to go and spread the Good News.

God commissions us through his Word. To understand and love the Word, we need the Spirit to illuminate our hearts.

Read Ephesians 1:13–14

- How do these two verses demonstrate how Word and Spirit go together?
- What does the Spirit do in these verses?

Prayer

Father, help us by your Spirit to understand your Word and follow what it says. May we repent and believe when we fail. Comfort our hearts by your Spirit and bring to mind all the promises in your Word that remind us of your grace and mercy. Thank you for your Spirit that drew us to you and assures us that we'll have eternity with you. We long for that day. In Jesus' name we pray. Amen.

DAY 3

The Spirit works through his people

> [8:29] And the Spirit said to Philip, "Go over and join this chariot." [30] So Philip ran to him and heard him reading Isaiah the prophet and asked, "Do you understand what you are reading?" [31] And he said, "How can I, unless someone guides me?" And he invited Philip to come up and sit with him.

Have you ever had someone give you tremendous help? Maybe it was on a tough homework assignment where you didn't know what to do and your parents came to your rescue. Perhaps your family was stuck on the side of the road, and some nice person stopped to give you a hand. Maybe you didn't have enough money to buy something you wanted, and you were able to do a little extra work for someone and get paid exactly what you needed to get what you wanted.

We all need help in various ways, and part of the joy of living in community is having people around us to give us help when we are in need.

The Spirit loves to do this when it comes to helping people understand his Word, the Bible. Think of all the ways that biblical explanation plays a role in our growth as Christians. We have preachers who speak to us from God's Word about the good news of Jesus and how it applies to our lives. We have small group leaders who facilitate discussion around God's Word so that we can encourage one another to grow in the grace and knowledge of God. We have close friends who help point us to God's Word as we walk through life together and endure various challenges along the way. We have various forms of media, including the Internet and podcasts, which explain the Bible to us.

God loves it when we seek to grow in our understanding of his Word. That is what we see here: Philip, compelled by the Spirit, is eager to explain God's Word, and the Ethiopian man is eager to learn.

Read Hebrews 3:12–14

- How often should we encourage one another with the Word?
- When we explain the Word to one another, how does it help us grow?
- How have you been encouraged in your life as the Ethiopian man was by Philip?

Prayer

Father, thank you that you provide so many different ways for us to learn and grow like the Ethiopian in this text. May we be eager to learn and grow like him. You have been so faithful to provide. Thank you, Father. In Jesus' name we pray. Amen.

DAY 4

The gospel preached in the Old Testament

[8:32] Now the passage of the Scripture that he was reading was this:

"Like a sheep he was led to the slaughter

and like a lamb before its shearer is silent,

so he opens not his mouth.

[33] In his humiliation justice was denied him.

Who can describe his generation?

For his life is taken away from the earth."

The Ethiopian man was reading a very famous passage of Scripture, a section from Isaiah 53, where the prophet Isaiah foretold of a servant of God who would lay down his life for others, sacrificing himself for their sins to make them clean. He would be obedient to God all the way to the end.

This text compares him to a sacrificial lamb, a symbol of atonement the Jewish people would have been very familiar with. Isaiah implies that the whole point of this sacrificial system was to point to the final sacrifice, the Lamb of God, Jesus, who would take away the sins of all those who come to him.

Isaiah's text also speaks of the justice that was denied Jesus. Jesus was perfect. He never sinned—not even once. So why would a perfect man be treated like the worst criminal ever? That is the pinnacle of injustice, right?

When you see the cross, you should be reminded that that is what our sin deserves. Thanks to God, Jesus bore the wrath of God for us. He was denied justice so that we could receive it. This is the most remarkable thing in the universe—that God would love us enough to do this for us. This is the gospel, and Isaiah 53 points forward to its reality.

Read 2 Corinthians 5:21

- How does this verse relate to our text above?
- How does the Old Testament sacrificial system point to Jesus?

Prayer

Father, we stand in awe of your justice and mercy. We thank you that you have provided a way for us to have our sins forgiven in Jesus. You are so amazing, and we want to worship you for your greatness. May we live our lives showing that we love you, have faith in you, and are thankful for what you have done for us. In Jesus' name we pray. Amen.

DAY 5

A godly teacher

[8:34] And the eunuch said to Philip, "About whom, I ask you, does the prophet say this, about himself or about someone else?" [35] Then Philip opened his mouth, and beginning with this Scripture he told him the good news about Jesus. [36] And as they were going along the road they came to some water, and the eunuch said, "See, here is water! What prevents me from being baptized?" [38] And he commanded the chariot to stop, and they both went down into the water, Philip and the eunuch, and he baptized him. [39] And when they came up out of the water, the Spirit of the Lord carried Philip away, and the eunuch saw him no more, and went on his way rejoicing. [40] But Philip found himself at Azotus, and as he passed through he preached the gospel to all the towns until he came to Caesarea.

Are you thankful for your teachers? Who have been some of your favorites teachers and why? What did they do that was so remarkable or impactful?

We all need good teachers in our lives. The Ethiopian eunuch had such a teacher in Philip, who taught him what the Old Testament was all about—Jesus the Messiah. Philip was so faithful in his teaching that God used it to draw this eunuch's heart to himself!

Hearing God's Word preached by a faithful teacher can be a great blessing, not only because it provides helpful instruction but because it helps us grow in our love for God and one another.

The lesson was life transforming for the Ethiopian eunuch, and it can be that way for us, too. Let's listen and learn with humble hearts.

Read 2 Timothy 3:15–16

- What do these verses say about teaching?
- What is the content that we are supposed to teach one another?
- What does this produce in us?

Prayer

Father, thank you that you use fallen human beings as your vehicles for truth. May you use us more and more in one another's lives to bless, instruct, and exhort. May this cause us to grow in our faith and see unbelievers come to the faith. In Jesus' name we pray. Amen.

WEEK 5

Acts 9:1–10

DAY 1

Persecution from Saul

> [9:1] But Saul, still breathing threats and murder against the dis-
> ciples of the Lord, went to the high priest [2] and asked him for
> letters to the synagogues at Damascus, so that if he found any
> belonging to the Way, men or women, he might bring them bound
> to Jerusalem.

Some people will always dislike Christians. In the US, it is rare to find someone murdered for their faith. But in other parts of the world, people are regularly murdered, tortured, stolen from, and experience a whole host of other horrible things because of their faith. Incidents like these are common in countries like North Korea, Sudan, Somalia, and Iraq.

Very early on in the history of the church, an individual named Saul led the effort to drive Christians into silence, hiding, prison, or worse. They posed a threat to the religious establishment of their day, and Saul was doing pretty well sitting atop that establishment.

So what did he do? The text says that he was "breathing threats and murder against the disciples of the Lord." In other words, he was spewing rage and mistreatment much like the town bully who just won't let up on his targets.

Do you know anyone like that?

Unfortunately, when God's Spirit draws people to himself, there is always backlash. So is it worth it to continue sharing the gospel? Of course! Enduring the wrath of man will be the means by which some of these will be rescued from the eternal wrath of God.

DAILY DEVOTIONS

Read Luke 21:17–19

- How does this verse relate to our reading for today?
- Have you ever been persecuted for your faith? What happened?
- How should we respond to persecution?

Prayer

Father, we need your help to endure persecution from those who hate us and for boldness in sharing our faith. We are tempted to shy away and fear trouble, but may you help us to love people enough to endure their hatred so that they may be won over by our testimony. In Jesus' name we pray. Amen.

DAY 2

Going to great lengths to persecute

> [9:1] But Saul, still breathing threats and murder against the disciples of the Lord, went to the high priest [2] and asked him for letters to the synagogues at Damascus, so that if he found any belonging to the Way, men or women, he might bring them bound to Jerusalem.

What are you willing to go to great lengths for? In your mind, what things are worth working really hard to obtain or achieve? Maybe it's a sports goal. Maybe it's an educational goal. Perhaps it's a promotion in your job. What is it for you?

Unfortunately, Saul was willing to go to great lengths to make sure that Christians would be thrown in prison. He truly hated them. He was a man of passion and his passionate pursuit was to do Christians harm.

We can see this clearly in today's text. Paul goes to the high priest, the one who called all the shots in Jewish matters, asking for his permission (this is why he asked for "letters") to hunt Christians worshiping Jesus in Damascus. Think of all that Paul had to do to go after the Christians—set up a meeting with the high priest, travel to Damascus by horse or foot while dodging danger, arrange travel plans for the Christians he had incarcerated, follow them on their journey to the authorities, and more!

But for Saul, it was well worth it. He felt that these Christians had to be stopped, and any trouble that he incurred in the process was no trouble at all.

Read Romans 8:18

- How is this verse a comfort when we are persecuted?
- Why is it difficult to think of eternal things in the midst of persecution?
- How should we respond to persecution?

Prayer

Father, may you cause those who persecute Christians to stop. But if they do not, give us the faith to endure. May our love for you be more passionate than their hatred. May a huge vision of eternity sustain us in our day-to-day troubles. Thank you that you did not flee from persecution but faced it willingly to save us. In Jesus' name we pray. Amen.

DAY 3

Persecuting the church is persecuting Jesus

[9:3] Now as he went on his way, he approached Damascus, and suddenly a light from heaven shone around him. [4] And falling to the ground he heard a voice saying to him, "Saul, Saul, why are you persecuting me?"

Have you ever been bullied? It's easy to hate the idea of bullying. For many parents the thought of their children being bullied at school produces in them a strong reaction. They hate to see their children bullied because there is nothing they love more in the world than their kids.

The same sentiment can be found in today's text. Did you notice something a bit unusual about the words that Paul hears while on his way to persecute the church? Jesus never mentions the church. Instead, he says, "Saul, Saul, why are you persecuting me?"

Isn't that interesting? In essence, Jesus equates Paul's attack on the church as an attack on him.

Why do you think that is?

The Bible refers to the church as "the body of Christ." Jesus actually indwells us both personally and collectively by his Spirit. By the power of the Spirit of Jesus that indwells us, the connection is so close that Jesus considers persecution of him and persecution of the church as one and the same! It's so good to know that Jesus loves the church as much as himself!

Read 1 Corinthians 3:16

- Why does this verse say that we are God's temple?
- If we are God's temple, that place where he dwells, can you see why God would hate persecution of the church?
- What does being God's temple mean for the way we live our lives?

Prayer

Father, thank you that you choose to indwell your people by your Spirit in the church. May we love the church like you love it. May your glory shine brightly as we model for the world what it means to love one another. In Jesus' name we pray. Amen.

DAY 4

God uses unlikely people

[9:5] And he said, "Who are you, Lord?" And he said, "I am Jesus, whom you are persecuting. [6] But rise and enter the city, and you will be told what you are to do." [7] The men who were traveling with him stood speechless, hearing the voice but seeing no one. [8] Saul rose from the ground, and although his eyes were opened, he saw nothing. So they led him by the hand and brought him into Damascus. [9] And for three days he was without sight, and neither ate nor drank.

Sometimes God uses the most unlikely of people to accomplish his mission. This is a common theme throughout the Bible.

God called out to Moses and told him to confront the most powerful man in the world at that time, Pharaoh, who was enslaving God's people. Moses had a big problem. He was a nobody, and he couldn't speak well. But God promised to be with him.

God told Joshua to lead his people into the promise land. There was a big problem, though: the people who lived there were very wicked and quite intimidating. The Israelites didn't really have a track record of being courageous and faithful; they were complainers and idolatrous. But God promised to be with him.

Gideon was a weak man from a weak family and people. God came to him and called him out to lead the effort against the Midianites who were oppressing God's people. Gideon was not a mighty warrior; in fact, he was a nobody. But God promised to be with him.

God loves to use the most unlikely of people to get his job done.

We see that again in today's text. Why would God want to use Paul? He was the number-one persecutor of the church. God loves to use people that we don't expect, because through such individuals we're convinced that it's his power at work and nothing else. So we give him the glory, instead of seeking it for ourselves.

Read 1 Corinthians 1:20–25

- What does this verse say about God using unlikely people?
- Were Moses, Joshua, Gideon, or Paul wise or significant in the world's eyes?
- Have you seen God use unlikely people in your life?

Prayer

Father, thank you that you use "nobodies" like us. We want your power and wisdom to shine through us. We want to make you famous by relying on your strength, not ours. May the world see that. In Jesus' name we pray. Amen.

DAILY DEVOTIONS

DAY 5

The dramatic awakening of God

[9:5] And he said, "Who are you, Lord?" And he said, "I am Jesus, whom you are persecuting. [6] But rise and enter the city, and you will be told what you are to do." [7] The men who were traveling with him stood speechless, hearing the voice but seeing no one. [8] Saul rose from the ground, and although his eyes were opened, he saw nothing. So they led him by the hand and brought him into Damascus. [9] And for three days he was without sight, and neither ate nor drank.

Have you ever had an experience that was quite jarring and abrupt? Maybe it was a car accident or a huge thunderclap that woke you up in the middle of the night. Perhaps it was a brother or sister who jumped out from behind a door to scare you. Maybe it was a sharp voice from one of your parents who caught you in the act of doing something you weren't supposed to.

Sometimes the Spirit moves us in subtle ways. Some people speak of a "still small voice" that moves us toward God. But sometimes he wakes us up through dramatic experiences, like in Paul's case—the Bible says that he was knocked to the ground and blinded!

When God draws individuals to himself, he often does so through a crisis at work, in relationships, or perhaps even through near-death experiences. You can be sure that God got Paul's attention and, if necessary, he can get ours, too.

Read John 6:44

- How do we see God drawing Paul to himself in this text?
- Do you know anyone who had a crisis that God used to draw their heart to him?

Prayer

Father, thank you that you sometimes use loud experiences to wake us up out of our sinful slumber. You love us too much to leave us alone; you're a Father who lovingly calls his children out of disobedience. You did it for Paul, and you do the same for us. May we be receptive to your call and to your correction. In Jesus' name we pray. Amen.

DAILY DEVOTIONS

WEEK 6

Acts 9:10–19a

DAY 1

A vision from God

> [9:10] Now there was a disciple at Damascus named Ananias. The Lord said to him in a vision, "Ananias." And he said, "Here I am, Lord." [11] And the Lord said to him, "Rise and go to the street called Straight, and at the house of Judas look for a man of Tarsus named Saul, for behold, he is praying, [12] and he has seen in a vision a man named Ananias come in and lay his hands on him so that he might regain his sight."

What is something that you've experienced recently that was out of the ordinary?

Today's text indicates that the disciple Ananias got a message loud and clear from God through something he saw and heard.

Without hesitating or running away, Ananias said, "Here I am, Lord!" He was willing to respond to the Lord's call.

This is a great model for us to follow when we read the Word of God. We too should say, "Here I am, Lord!" before we delve into it. Then, with that kind of attitude, we'll be ready and able to respond to whatever we find in it.

Read Hebrews 1:1–3

- According to this text, how does God speak to us?
- Where do we find Jesus speaking?
- Why is it important to regularly listen for God's voice?

Prayer

Father, thank you that you still communicate with us through your Word, through creation, and in other unique ways. May we be willing to listen and obey to whatever you say. Thank you for loving us enough to leave us your message. In Jesus' name we pray. Amen.

DAY 2

Carry my name

> [9:13] But Ananias answered, "Lord, I have heard from many about this man, how much evil he has done to your saints at Jerusalem. [14] And here he has authority from the chief priests to bind all who call on your name." [15] But the Lord said to him, "Go, for he is a chosen instrument of mine to carry my name before the Gentiles and kings and the children of Israel."

Do you play an instrument? If so, what do you play? What do you love about it? Does the instrument do anything without you picking it up? Does it ever just jump up out of the case all by itself and start playing a festive little tune?

Of course not. One of the things that make an instrument an instrument is that you're able to make it do what you want it to do. The piano just sits there until someone sits down and decides to make it sound a certain way.

In today's text, we learn that Paul is the piano, and God is about to sit down and use him to play some very beautiful music. Before this, Satan was the player. Now God has taken over this "chosen instrument" to bring his message to all the nations.

We should all pray that God would use us like this. May we simply be the Lord's instrument. May he play the beautiful music of the gospel through our lives.

Read Colossians 1:28–29

- How do these verses show that Paul is being used by God?
- What is Paul's goal?
- How does he do that?

Prayer

Father, may we be your chosen instruments just like Paul. We want to be used by you to make disciples for your glory. Help us to forsake our sin and run to you so that we can be faithful. There is no greater joy than knowing we are being used by you for your purposes. In Jesus' name we pray. Amen.

DAY 3

Suffering for Jesus

[9:16] "For I will show him how much he must suffer for the sake of my name."

One of the challenges of being a follower of Jesus is the reality of suffering. Jesus promised that his followers would experience persecution if they were faithful to him—meaning, some would seek their destruction.

In today's text, God tells Ananias that this would be true of Paul. He would become one of the most faithful servants that the church would ever see: He would write over half of the New Testament. He would travel thousands of miles to preach the gospel to the unreached. He would endure numerous trials that included bad weather, fierce animals, and wicked people. And like Jesus, Paul too would experience suffering's bittersweetness.

We live in a fallen world infected with sin, and we serve a God who was brutally murdered. We will suffer, but the reason for suffering is often mysterious and unknowable. God is a good Father who does not desire suffering for his children (2 Pet. 3:9), but he is also a powerful Sovereign who can take the worst of suffering and redeem it according to his good purpose. This was certainly the case for Paul, and this was certainly the case for Jesus.

Read 2 Timothy 3:12

- Why would godliness lead to persecution?
- Have you ever suffered for Jesus?
- How can we endure suffering for Jesus in our day and age?

Prayer

Father, we know that suffering is simply a part of the Christian life. We know that if we are faithful in telling others the truth about Jesus, sin, and salvation, there will be some who hate the message. Help us to love even when we are hated. Help us to pray for those who hurt us. Give us wisdom to use our words well so that the message is the only thing that offends, and not our behavior. In Jesus' name we pray. Amen.

DAY 4

Paul receives the Spirit

> [9:17] So Ananias departed and entered the house. And laying his hands on him he said, "Brother Saul, the Lord Jesus who appeared to you on the road by which you came has sent me so that you may regain your sight and be filled with the Holy Spirit."

One of the most important aspects of a faithful ministry is the active involvement of the Holy Spirit. We have seen this over and over again in the book of Acts, and it is reaffirmed here in verse 17. Before Paul was used by God to do all the amazing things he would do, he was "filled with the Holy Spirit."

Why do you think this was the case?

It's kind of like a car. Does your car work all by itself, or are there certain conditions that have to be met before you take off down the road? What are some of those conditions? Of course, one essential thing your car needs in order to run smoothly on the highway is gas. No gas, no trip. What happens if the car runs out of gas? You stop. The road trip is over.

It's kind of like that with the Holy Spirit. The Holy Spirit is the fuel for ministry. He is the power to make the engine run. If we are going to travel all over the world to share the good news of Jesus, we have to make sure our gas tank is filled with the power of the Holy Spirit. Without it, we're sunk.

Fortunately, God is a good Father who loves to give good gifts to his children. The number-one gift that he loves to give is himself in the form of this

Holy Spirit. Isn't that good news? Before he set out to accomplish great things through God's power, Paul was equipped.

Read Galatians 5:22–23

- What does being Spirit-filled look like?
- Who in your life appears to be filled with the Spirit?
- As you hear the list of the fruits of the Spirit, which one strikes you as the one you need to grow in?

Prayer

Father, thank you that promise to give the Holy Spirit to those who believe in you and want to follow you. May your power shine through us graciously to unbelievers and believers alike. May we be loving, joyful, and filled with all the other fruits of your Spirit. In Jesus' name we pray. Amen.

DAY 5

Rising to be baptized

[9:18] And immediately something like scales fell from his eyes, and he regained his sight. Then he rose and was baptized; [19] and taking food, he was strengthened.

Once Paul received the Spirit, what was the first thing he did?

The text says that he rose and "was baptized." Why do you think that was important for him to do? Why do you think that was the first thing he did?

Throughout Acts, we see how important the practice of baptism is. Once there is the realization that Jesus is Lord, one follows up that conviction with being baptized, which publicly declares allegiance to Jesus. The believer descends under water and is buried with him in his death. Jesus' death becomes a death he died for them. When the believer ascends from the water, they are "raised to walk in newness of life" (Rom. 6:4). They are empowered by the Spirit to live their lives for his glory.

This was true of Paul. That's why his first act as a Christian was to be baptized.

Read Romans 6:1–4

- Why is unrepentant sin not an option for the believer?
- What does baptism symbolize and why is it important?
- Why can we walk in newness of life when we become a Christian?

Prayer

Father, thank you that you have given us this powerful symbol called baptism. May we remember ourselves as those who have been given all that is true of Jesus: we are spiritually united to him in his death, and death no longer has mastery over us because he conquered it. Thank you, Father, for allowing us to live in this reality. In Jesus' name we pray. Amen.

WEEK 7

Acts 9:19b–31

DAY 1

A radical change

[9:19b] For some days he was with the disciples at Damascus. [20] And immediately he proclaimed Jesus in the synagogues, saying, "He is the Son of God." [21] And all who heard him were amazed and said, "Is not this the man who made havoc in Jerusalem of those who called upon this name? And has he not come here for this purpose, to bring them bound before the chief priests?" [22] But Saul increased all the more in strength, and confounded the Jews who lived in Damascus by proving that Jesus was the Christ.

Imagine the worst of all playground bullies. He is focused in his cruelty and preys on the weaker kids, who bear the brunt of his taunts, threats, and fists. He is also smart enough to know how to bully the other kids in ways that hurt them without any teacher or administrator at the school ever finding out what was happening.

Now imagine this same bully comes to school one day with gifts for everyone. He hands out compliments like he used to hand out sucker punches to the midsection. He is perfectly respectful and calm at all times.

What would you think?

You might think that he was up to something even more sinister, right? "Why is he buttering everyone up?" you might think to yourself.

Well, this is kind of what happened in the life of Paul. Today's text makes that clear. People didn't know what to do with him! The Jews couldn't understand why he was testifying about Christ, and the Christians couldn't figure it out why he was no longer threatening them or throwing them in jail.

Sometimes when God draws us to himself through the gospel, there's confusion for a bit while people try to figure out what's going on with us. This was certainly the case with Paul.

Read 2 Corinthians 5:17

- How do you see the truth of this verse in the life of Paul?
- Can you think of anyone else in your life or at church that has become a "new creation"?

Prayer

Father, thank you that you truly change people. May we be thankful that we are not what we once were. May you give us a greater desire for holiness. May we see more and more people coming to know you and feeling the true joy of the abundant life. In Jesus' name we pray. Amen.

DAY 2

Attempted murder

[9:23] When many days had passed, the Jews plotted to kill him, [24] but their plot became known to Saul. They were watching the gates day and night in order to kill him, [25] but his disciples took him by night and let him down through an opening in the wall, lowering him in a basket.

Sometimes being a Christian is downright dangerous. In today's text, we see that there was a plot to kill Saul by people who didn't appreciate his message.

Thankfully, Saul found out about it, and his friends helped him to escape.

You'd think that if people were plotting to kill you, you might be doing something wrong. But with Saul, that was not the case. Can you think of anyone else in the Bible whom people plotted to kill because they hated his message?

Jesus is the first person that comes to mind. If you read the Gospels, you'll see Jesus treated in a fashion very similar to Paul's. People hated his message, they viewed him as a threat, and then they plotted to kill him.

But oftentimes in the Gospels, we read that "they could not touch him" because his appointed time had not yet come (John 7:30). What this means is that hovering above the plotting of wicked men is the sovereignty of God. No one could touch Jesus or Saul apart from the will of God.

Let that be a comfort for you. God controls all things, so live wisely, yet fearlessly.

Read John 7:30

- How do we see the sovereignty of God in this verse?
- How can this verse be a comfort for you?
- How have you seen the sovereignty of God in your life?

Prayer

Father, thank you that you order our lives by your sovereignty. Help us to live fearlessly for your glory. Rescue us when we are in danger while helping us to remember that you hold us eternally, and death will have no victory over us. Thank you, Father. In Jesus' name we pray. Amen.

DAY 3

Preaching Jesus

[9:26] And when he had come to Jerusalem, he attempted to join the disciples. And they were all afraid of him, for they did not believe that he was a disciple. [27] But Barnabas took him and brought him to the apostles and declared to them how on the road he had seen the Lord, who spoke to him, and how at Damascus he had preached boldly in the name of Jesus.

Is there anything you would die for?

Let's say that you went around telling everyone that you loved a certain band, but this wasn't true. Everyone else seemed to love this band, so you wanted to follow along.

Now, would you say this if your life depended on telling the truth?

The text says that Saul "preached boldly in the name of Jesus." Why would this be the thing that would convince people that Saul was worthy to be trusted? The answer is because back then if you were "preaching boldly" for Jesus' sake, it was kind of like inviting a gun to your head. You might lose your life for it. In fact, people were trying to kill Saul!

In Barnabas' mind, there is no way that Saul would put his life on the line by preaching, unless he really believed the message to be true! People don't usually die for something they know is not true.

May we have the same confidence and faith to preach boldly like Saul, even if the cost is very high.

Read 2 Timothy 4:1–2

- Why is bold preaching important?
- Why would Saul's preaching prove that he was truly a Christian?

Prayer

Father, give us the boldness to preach like Saul, no matter the consequences. May people be awakened to faith in Jesus because of our faithfulness in sharing the truth about his life, death, resurrection, and return. Help us, by your Spirit, to be bold. In Jesus' name we pray. Amen.

DAY 4

A time to stay and a time to flee

[9:28] So he went in and out among them at Jerusalem, preaching boldly in the name of the Lord. [29] And he spoke and disputed against the Hellenists. But they were seeking to kill him. [30] And

DAILY DEVOTIONS

when the brothers learned this, they brought him down to Caesarea
and sent him off to Tarsus.

We have learned that persecution is simply a fact of the Christian life. If we are
being a faithful witness to the life, death, and resurrection of Jesus, there will
always be people who don't like this and, if we continue to speak, will persecute
us in ways big or small.

Sometimes it's hard to know how to deal with this. Should we stay, or
should we flee?

In the Bible, we see both responses. Jesus knew when it was time to retreat
from persecution, and he knew when it was time to stay and ready himself for
whatever would come. As a result, he was eventually killed for choosing not to
run from his persecutors—and this was all part of God's plan.

The book of Acts paints a similar picture. When Peter and John were
persecuted for their preaching, they didn't run and hide but said, "We cannot
but speak of what we have seen and heard" (Acts 4:20). They refused to shut
up about Jesus and, as a result, endured a beating from the religious rulers.

But in this text, we also learn that there is a time to run from persecution.
Paul did just that. With the help of his friends, he retreated from a situation that
threatened his life. But interestingly, he did so without changing his approach
to ministry in the least; he simply continued to preach in a new location to a
new group of people without hesitation.

So, when is it good to endure persecution and when is it good to flee
it? There is no easy answer to this question. Certainly it implies prayerful
wisdom and conversation with others who love you, love God, and love his
mission in the world. Either way, our declaration of the truth about Jesus
shouldn't stop.

Read Romans 8:35–39

- How is this verse a comfort for us when we're persecuted?
- Amid persecution, do you think you'd stay or flee?
- When would it be important to stay?

Prayer

Father, we need wisdom to do the right thing when we are persecuted. Help us to know which way to turn. We just want to be faithful. May you be glorified in our actions. May you draw more and more people to yourself. In Jesus' name we pray. Amen.

DAY 5

Walking in fear and comfort

> [9:31] So the church throughout all Judea and Galilee and Samaria had peace and was being built up. And walking in the fear of the Lord and in the comfort of the Holy Spirit, it multiplied.

What is the key to growing a church? How does a church remain healthy amid various challenges? We have learned in the book of Acts that the church had to endure various forms of persecution: Peter and John were beaten for preaching. Stephen was stoned to death. Paul was dragged off to prison.

Today's text says that the church was "being built up." How could that have happened in light of such circumstances?

The text gives us two clues: it says that they were walking in the fear of the Lord and in the comfort of the Holy Spirit. Why do you think those two things would cause them to grow in spite of all these challenges?

Walking in the fear of the Lord means that they feared God more than they feared their attackers. This gave them immense power to endure whatever came their way. In addition, they were comforted by the Holy Spirit. The Holy Spirit was alive in them, and he brought to mind all of God's promises about a future resurrection and their hope beyond this life.

In light of these truths, they could be fearless, and this fearlessness produced in them a willingness to speak and to serve. Usually, when this happens among God's people, the church multiplies. This is what happened in the book of Acts. We should pray that it happens among us today as well.

DAILY DEVOTIONS

Read Matthew 10:28–31

- How do these verses remind you of the people in the book of Acts?
- Identify the warning and the promise in these verses.
- Why do the fear of the Lord and the comfort of the Holy Spirit grow the church?

Prayer

Father, may we fear you and know your comfort by the power of your Holy Spirit. When we face trials of various kinds, may we count it all joy to endure for the glory of your name. May you grow your church through our testimony. In Jesus' name we pray. Amen.

WEEK 8

Acts 9:32–43

DAY 1

Giving credit where credit is due

> [9:32] Now as Peter went here and there among them all, he came down also to the saints who lived at Lydda. [33] There he found a man named Aeneas, bedridden for eight years, who was paralyzed. [34] And Peter said to him, "Aeneas, Jesus Christ heals you; rise and make your bed." And immediately he rose. [35] And all the residents of Lydda and Sharon saw him, and they turned to the Lord.

Where does the electrical power in your home come from? Does it just come magically out of the ground and then flow into your house?

No, it's not magic; it's electricity. It usually comes into your house from wires that run along telephone poles or underground. The electricity draws its power from a huge power source somewhere in the city. There would be no electrical power in your home apart from this source.

In today's text, Peter says something very interesting about the healing that he performs. He says, "Jesus Christ heals you," despite the fact that you would have only seen Peter and a man named Aeneas in the room. Why didn't Peter just say, "Aeneas, today I heal you"?

Peter said what he did because he knew that the power to heal came from a source other than himself. He was simply giving credit where credit was due. Just like your house owes its electrical power to a source outside of it, Peter owes his power to a source outside of himself. He knew that the power to heal anyone had to come through the Spirit of Jesus flowing through him.

Read John 15:1–5

- How is fruit born in the life of a Christian?
- What can we do to allow Jesus to empower us?

Prayer

Father, empower us to do mighty deeds in your name. May the world take notice of you working through us. May we be quick to acknowledge your power working in and through us. We need your help to do this. In Jesus' name we pray. Amen.

DAY 2

Seeing is believing

[9:32] Now as Peter went here and there among them all, he came down also to the saints who lived at Lydda. [33] There he found a man named Aeneas, bedridden for eight years, who was paralyzed. [34] And Peter said to him, "Aeneas, Jesus Christ heals you; rise and make your bed." And immediately he rose. [35] And all the residents of Lydda and Sharon saw him, and they turned to the Lord.

Have you ever gone fishing? What are the important aspects of being a good fisherman? A good pole? A good bucket? A good boat?

All of these things are very important, but perhaps the most important is having the right bait. You have to have way to draw in the fish.

God uses various means to draw people to himself, and one of the ways we see in this text is through the use of miracles. We learn in verse 35 that dozens, if not hundreds, of people saw this man healed by Jesus through Peter. They had to be asking themselves, "How did this happen?" Their curiosity would have carved a path for them to hear about the power of Jesus to save.

Not all people who witness miracles will be saved, but many times it can be a thing that God uses to overcome our hardness of heart. We should pray for miracles to happen in our day and that this would make believers out of unbelievers.

Read Matthew 5:14–16

- What are the benefits of showing others our good works?
- What kinds of good works could you do in public that might draw people closer to Jesus?
- What could happen if we're showing others our good works not for God's glory but for personal gain?

Prayer

Father, may we continue to see people come to faith through your miracles. But at the same time, may normal acts of Christian love be enough. May we be bold to tell others how your Spirit is working in us. Please use us to draw people to you. In Jesus' name we pray. Amen.

DAY 3

The comfort of godly leadership

[9:36] Now there was in Joppa a disciple named Tabitha, which, translated, means Dorcas. She was full of good works and acts of charity. [37] In those days she became ill and died, and when they had washed her, they laid her in an upper room. [38] Since Lydda was near Joppa, the disciples, hearing that Peter was there, sent two men to him, urging him, "Please come to us without delay."

Have you ever been in a really dire situation?

Today's text describes how some of God's people were placed in a very difficult situation: one of their good friends and fellow servants had died.

Sometimes when we are in such situations, we can feel a bit desperate. We need help, but oftentimes we feel so hopeless. This is simply part of the human experience, felt by many people and written about by the psalmists, Jeremiah, and Job.

DAILY DEVOTIONS

One of the things that can help us experience a great deal of comfort in the face of death and loss is the presence of a godly leader, whose gentle presence can remind us of God's truth. Peter was such a leader, used mightily by God to bring great comfort to God's people.

We should be thankful for people in our lives who can help us in our times of need. This might be your parents, your grandparents, your pastors, or your mentors/teachers. God has structured our lives to lean on one another, especially when our trials are really difficult.

Read 2 Corinthians 2:3–8

- How and why does God comfort us?
- Who would you want nearby if you were enduring something really difficult? Why?
- How can you be a comfort to others?

Prayer

Father, thank you that you use others to comfort us in our trials. May we be a blessing to others when they are in need. We know that even if things in this life remain challenging, there will come a day when you will make all things right. In Jesus' name we pray. Amen.

DAY 4

Prayer and miracles

[9:39] So Peter rose and went with them. And when he arrived, they took him to the upper room. All the widows stood beside him weeping and showing tunics and other garments that Dorcas made while she was with them. [40] But Peter put them all out-side, and knelt down and prayed; and turning to the body he said, "Tabitha, arise." And she opened her eyes, and when she saw Peter she sat up.

In today's text, we see a powerful combination: prayer and miracles. Why do you think those two things go well together?

One reason is that God wants us to express our need for him, and he desires to meet that need. When this happens, he is glorified (i.e., seen as beautiful and worthy of trust).

In this text, Peter shows up at the bedside of Dorcas. The first thing he does is pray. We don't have a record of what he said, but we can be sure that he prayed to raise this woman from the dead for the sake of God's name.

Sometimes, God chooses to answer prayers like this, and unimaginable, miraculous events take place. We should never be afraid to ask God to move in powerful ways like this!

Of course, all of these things are true regardless of whether God performs a miracle through our prayers or not. Sometimes, God chooses to show his power in ways that amazes us. Let's pray boldly for a miracle like Peter and be truly thankful when he provides!

Read John 11:38–44

- Why did Jesus pray before he performed this miracle?
- What is similar about this passage to Acts 9:39–40?
- Have you ever seen or heard about miracles in response to bold praying?

Prayer

Father, help us to have the confidence to be able to pray bold prayers like those we see from Jesus and Peter. May you do miracles in our day. May you cause people to come to know you through them. May you help us in our unbelief. We know that apart from you we can do nothing. Draw near to us as we draw near to you. In Jesus' name we pray. Amen.

DAY 5

Front-page news

[9:41] And he gave her his hand and raised her up. Then calling the saints and widows, he presented her alive. [42] And it became known throughout all Joppa, and many believed in the Lord. [43] And he stayed in Joppa for many days with one Simon, a tanner.

What do you think the term "front-page news" means?

We don't live in a world that is dominated by newspapers anymore. Most people forty and younger now get their news via the Internet. But twenty years ago, it was different. The daily newspaper was central in our culture; it was one of the main ways by which important information was spread throughout our nation and world.

News that was considered vitally important was on the front page because it would be the first thing that people saw when they picked up the newspaper. Famous front-page headlines throughout our American history include the bombing of Pearl Harbor, the assassination of President JFK, and the 9/11 terrorist attacks.

When news hits the front page, it travels fast.

According to our text, what Peter did made the front page during the first-century world. The news of God raising Dorcas from the dead through Peter traveled to the whole town. What was the news' effect?

"Many people believed in the Lord."

No matter what, we should be the kind of people who are ready and willing to acknowledge King Jesus as the one who is truly newsworthy. His resurrection is the most newsworthy event the world has ever seen. In fact, the word gospel means "good news." It's as important as any headline we'll see on the front page.

Read Mark 1:14–15

- The word "gospel" in this text could also be translated "good news." What was the "news" that Jesus came to bring?
- Was this news a big deal for Jesus? If so, why?

Prayer

Father, thank you that you have declared the best news in the world through your Son Jesus. May this "front page news" be heard in all corners of the world. We know that has not happened yet, but use us, your church, to spread this news to all peoples and nations. In Jesus' name we pray. Amen.

WEEK 9

Acts 10:1–48

DAY 1

Devoted to God, a mission from God

[10:1] At Caesarea there was a man named Cornelius, a centurion of what was known as the Italian Cohort, [2] a devout man who feared God with all his household, gave alms generously to the people, and prayed continually to God. [3] About the ninth hour of the day he saw clearly in a vision an angel of God come in and say to him, "Cornelius." [4] And he stared at him in terror and said, "What is it, Lord?" And he said to him, "Your prayers and your alms have ascended as a memorial before God. [5] And now send men to Joppa and bring one Simon who is called Peter. [6] He is lodging with one Simon, a tanner, whose house is by the sea." [7] When the angel who spoke to him had departed, he called two of his servants and a devout soldier from among those who attended him, [8] and having related everything to them, he sent them to Joppa.

At the beginning of this text, we learn about a Roman centurion named Cornelius, who was in charge of 100 soldiers in the Roman military. He was a man who understood leadership and warfare. He was likely not easily intimidated by much of anything, but we learn in these verses that he was terrified of something. Do you remember what it was?

It was a vision from God that he received. If an angel from heaven visibly came to you to bring a command, you'd probably be pretty terrified as well. That's not something that happens every day!

The tough guy is humbled by what he saw and heard, but we also learn something very interesting about Cornelius—namely, that he was man of prayer. More interestingly, the angel tells him that God had heard his prayers. Isn't that cool?

Sometimes when we draw near to God, he will give us a specific mission or calling. This was the case for Cornelius. He was going to have an important role to play in the life of Peter, and this would have a huge impact on the future of Christianity. We might not get to do something like Cornelius, but everyone has a calling from God that is made manifest when we draw near to him.

Read James 4:7–8

- Why could it seem like God is far away when we insist on being far away from him?
- What is one way you could devote yourself to God today?

Prayer

Father, thank you that you choose to use us in your plan for the world. Help us to draw near to you and away from sin. We want to be a blessing for the kingdom. In Jesus' name we pray. Amen.

DAY 2

Clean and unclean

[10:9] The next day, as they were on their journey and approaching the city, Peter went up on the housetop about the sixth hour to pray. [10] And he became hungry and wanted something to eat, but while they were preparing it, he fell into a trance [11] and saw the heavens opened and something like a great sheet descending, being let down by its four corners upon the earth. [12] In it were all kinds of animals and reptiles and birds of the air. [13] And there came a voice to him: "Rise, Peter; kill and eat." [14] But Peter said, "By no means, Lord; for I have never eaten anything that is common or unclean." [15] And the voice came to him again a second time, "What God has made clean, do not call common." [16] This happened three times, and the thing was taken up at once to heaven.

"Go clean your room!" Have you ever heard these words from your parents? Having the house clean is very important to many people. It helps us find things, not get sick, and maintain the value of the property.

For someone like Peter, a first-century Jewish Christian, cleanliness was very important, too. But for people like him, cleanliness had nothing to do with dusting, vacuum cleaners, or toilet brushes, but more to do with the type of foods they ate and the people they associated with, as commanded in the Old Testament.

But all that was about to change. And it started with a vision that Peter received from God, in which he is commanded to kill and eat animals, which tradition had deemed "unclean." But they were now good for food. Symbolically, the vision was declaring that the Jewish people could now confidently accept the Gentiles into the community of faith.

Their new mission would demand that they evangelize people from all over the world. The days of separation were over.

Read Galatians 3:28

- What does this verse have to do with today's text?
- Who is welcome to come to Jesus? Is anyone excluded? Why is this an important question to ask?

Prayer

Father, thank you for paving a way for the whole world to come to you. We want to believe with Peter that all peoples of the earth are worthy to hear the message of Jesus. We don't want our religious traditions to get in the way of your mission's progress. Help us be faithful. In Jesus' name we pray. Amen.

DAY 3

The importance of being a witness

[10:34] So Peter opened his mouth and said: "Truly I understand that God shows no partiality, [35] but in every nation anyone who fears him and does what is right is acceptable to him. [36] As for the word that he sent to Israel, preaching good news of peace through Jesus Christ (he is Lord of all), [37] you yourselves know what happened throughout all Judea, beginning from Galilee after the baptism that John proclaimed: [38] how God anointed Jesus of Nazareth with the Holy Spirit and with power. He went about doing good and healing all who were oppressed by the devil, for God was with him. [39] And we are witnesses of all that he did both in the country of the Jews and in Jerusalem. They put him to death by hanging him on a tree."

Today's text jumps ahead a few verses. Let's summarize the verses that we skipped.

At Cornelius' request, Peter travels to his home. Cornelius is so honored to have him there that he tries to bow down and worship him. Peter does not allow this and reminds him that he, too, is simply a man like himself.

Now, in these verses, Peter shares the gospel with the people who had gathered at Cornelius' home. One of the important facets of his summary of the gospel is the fact that he and many others were witnesses. In essence, he is saying, "You can trust every word that I say. I saw it with my own eyes." This is important because it goes beyond just saying that he had a deep feeling about Jesus or that he even had a singular vision about Jesus—he actually experienced the risen Jesus in flesh and blood, and this same experience happened to many others.

Our faith is grounded not on the testimony of just one person with one experience, but on the testimony of many people sharing the same experience of a physically raised Jesus.

DAILY DEVOTIONS

If your message is a lie, and someone tells you to stop speaking about it or they'll kill you, you'd probably stop speaking. But that's not what happened here. The witnesses kept speaking and eventually gave their lives for it. This is evidence of the truth, and our faith is based on it.

Read 1 Corinthians 15:3–8

- What does this verse have to do with our text and devotional today?
- Why is the testimony of these eyewitnesses important for our faith?

Prayer

Father, thank you that you sent Peter to speak the gospel to Cornelius and his family and friends. We know that had this not taken place, we would not have received the gospel. Thank you that your message is for all nations and peoples and that its testimony is true. In Jesus' name we pray. Amen.

DAY 4

Judge of the living and the dead

[10:40] "But God raised him on the third day and made him to appear, [41] not to all the people but to us who had been chosen by God as witnesses, who ate and drank with him after he rose from the dead. [42] And he commanded us to preach to the people and to testify that he is the one appointed by God to be judge of the living and the dead. [43] To him all the prophets bear witness that everyone who believes in him receives forgiveness of sins through his name."

"Don't judge me!"

It's a phrase that's thrown around quite a bit in our culture. We all hate the thought that someone might look at our lives and judge us. It makes us feel uncomfortable, alienated, and exposed. It can sound like we're being put down, and we all hate feeling that way.

There certainly are real dangers in expressing to someone that their behavior is wrong. Our tone of voice and choice of words are important, and we need to be very careful, lest we fall into sin in the process of exposing sin. Our desire should be repentance on the part of the person in sin.

But there is one person who has every right to expose our sin. He has no chance of ever being wrong in his assessment. He never runs the danger of being a hypocrite. He never has to second-guess if he should speak or not. That person is Jesus. There is coming a day when he will judge all the living and the dead as today's text declares.

We know that he is the person who will do this because he triumphantly rose from the dead. This is the sign that Jesus is Lord! This is Peter's point in his message to Cornelius.

There is hope on the Day of Judgment. Anyone who has trusted and followed Jesus will be safe from his wrath on that day.

Read John 12:47–48

- What will be the basis for Jesus' judgment?
- Do you fear the judgment of God?
- What is your hope for the Day of Judgment?

Prayer

Father, you are the King. We want to submit to your rule. We want to align ourselves to what you say is right and be against what you say is wrong. Help us to know and love the difference. Thank you for providing a way of escape on the Day of Judgment. May we never take it for granted. In Jesus' name we pray. Amen.

DAY 5

Surprise, Jesus is for everyone!

[10:44] While Peter was still saying these things, the Holy Spirit fell on all who heard the word. [45] And the believers from among

DAILY DEVOTIONS

the circumcised who had come with Peter were amazed, because the gift of the Holy Spirit was poured out even on the Gentiles. [46] For they were hearing them speaking in tongues and extolling God. Then Peter declared, [47] "Can anyone withhold water for baptizing these people, who have received the Holy Spirit just as we have?" [48] And he commanded them to be baptized in the name of Jesus Christ. Then they asked him to remain for some days.

Has God ever shown you something in his Word that totally changed your opinion about something? Have you ever been corrected by someone and, in the process, began seeing that your way of thinking was wrong? There is something strangely freeing about seeing things in a new way and knowing that the old way is gone forever.

In this text, Jesus' Jewish followers experienced something similar. Knowing they were God's chosen people, they thought that the Messiah had come for them and them only. What they didn't expect was that the Gentiles would be included in God's plan of salvation. The text says they were "amazed."

God welcomes all to come to him and find salvation, regardless of skin color, background, or country of origin. May this truth free us to see the good news of Jesus reach all nations!

Read Revelation 7:9–10

- How do these two verses support the point of our devotional for today?
- Why do you think God loves people of all nations?

Prayer

Father, thank you for allowing all to come to Jesus. Thank you that we have the freedom to declare your grace to anyone and everyone under the sun. We want to have an attitude toward all peoples that is inclusive and loving. Help us to never see our heritage or ethnicity as a source of pride. May it never be a barrier to our witness for you. In Jesus' name we pray. Amen.

WEEK 10

Acts 11:1–18

DAY 1

Resistance to the movement of God

> [11:1] Now the apostles and the brothers who were throughout Judea
> heard that the Gentiles also had received the word of God. [2] So
> when Peter went up to Jerusalem, the circumcision party criticized
> him, saying, [3] "You went to uncircumcised men and ate with
> them."

Some people hate change. Are you one of them? Is change hard for you? Do you get nervous and desire a quick return to the way things used to be?

For many (especially those in the church), change can be very challenging, especially when it looms on the horizon. They might ask, "Are you sure we should be doing this?" to question the motives for change, to blatantly resist, or to incite others to join them.

Sadly, this happens in many businesses, civic organizations, and churches. It also happened when God ushered in a whole new era, inviting outsiders into his redemptive plan.

We have learned throughout Acts that God was starting something completely new through the Holy Spirit. We learned about this last week in the account of Peter and Cornelius. As we move on to chapter 11, we learn that not everyone was excited about the fact that other people groups were being allowed into the community of faith—the "circumcision party" condemned Peter for visiting the house of a Gentile.

There will always be resistance to the movement of God. Sometimes God calls his people to lead out and change things from the way they have always been. We need not fear change because God goes with us into the unknown future and promises to never leave or forsake us.

Read Isaiah 41:10

- How can this verse be a comfort for us when people resist change?
- List some of the downsides of never changing anything in our churches.

Prayer

Father, thank you that never allow people to hinder your ultimate plans. We don't want to resist, but we want to be on board with what you would have for us as we move into the future. Help us to know how to wisely navigate through change and bring the most glory to you in the process. In Jesus' name we pray. Amen.

DAY 2

A vision from God

> [11:4] But Peter began and explained it to them in order: [5] "I was in the city of Joppa praying, and in a trance I saw a vision, something like a great sheet descending, being let down from heaven by its four corners, and it came down to me. [6] Looking at it closely, I observed animals and beasts of prey and reptiles and birds of the air. [7] And I heard a voice saying to me, 'Rise, Peter; kill and eat.'"

Isn't it amazing that the God of the universe, the one who spoke the stars into existence, pulled the mountains out of the grounds, and said to the oceans, "Thus far shall you come and no farther" (Job 38:11), would choose to communicate with us through the Bible?

While knowledge about God, his people, and his mission can be found in his Word, we see that sometimes God uses dreams and visions to confirm it, as he does in Acts 11. Here, God gives Peter a vision, telling him to kill and eat some animals the Jewish tradition had said was "unclean." It didn't matter anymore, though: God was saying they were good enough to eat!

But far beyond changing rules about food, God was using the symbolic vision to say something more profound: the once "unclean" Gentiles were good enough to include in the community of faith.

Interestingly, Peter's vision wasn't a new revelation. In fact, God had declared the Gentiles' inclusion through the prophets hundreds of years earlier (cf. Isa. 42:6; 49:6). His vision is unlike many other modern-day ones, which claim a word from God but don't have a footing in God's Word.

Visions that are really from God don't contradict his Word; they merely underscore its truth. Peter's vision fulfilled Old Testament prophecies, showing that God had indeed communicated all of it to us before in his Word.

Read Matthew 4:4

- How can we normally expect to hear from God?
- This verse says that our very life flows from God's Word because it is food for the soul. Do you feel hungry?

Prayer

Father, thank you that you communicated with Peter in this unique way. We trust that you know what is best. We thank you for your Word and the fact that you meet us in it. We thank you that we can know you through it and that it provides for us the message of salvation. We are so thankful for this precious gift. In Jesus' name we pray. Amen.

DAY 3

Declare!

[11:6] "Looking at it closely, I observed animals and beasts of prey and reptiles and birds of the air. [7] And I heard a voice saying to me, 'Rise, Peter; kill and eat.' [8] But I said, 'By no means, Lord; for nothing common or unclean has ever entered my mouth.' [9] But the voice answered a second time from heaven, 'What God has made clean, do not call common.' [10] This happened three times, and all was drawn up again into heaven. [11] And behold, at that very moment three men arrived at the house in which we were, sent to me from Caesarea. [12] And the Spirit told me to go with them, making no distinction. These six brothers also accompanied me, and we entered the man's house. [13] And he told us how he had seen the angel stand in his house and say, 'Send to Joppa and bring Simon who is called Peter; [14] he will declare to you a message by which you will be saved, you and all your household.'"

Today's text should be familiar because Peter is simply recounting what we learned had happened to him in chapter 10. This text is rather long, but let's focus on one simple word because of its many implications for us: "declare."

We should notice that the angel said to Cornelius that Peter would bring a message to "declare." It may seem painfully obvious, but sadly, in our world today, some Christians don't believe that declaring the gospel is that important. They believe that we should simply love people through good deeds, and if they happen to ask us about our faith we might tell them, but we should never go out of our way to declare to anyone that they need to repent of their sin, trust God's gift of salvation in Jesus, and follow Jesus. This is just not true.

Notice in the last verse of our text that the word "declare" precedes "saved." This implies that no one gets saved apart from the verbal declaration of the gospel. We can love people with good deeds until we are blue in the face, but at some point, we have to declare the message just like Peter did to Cornelius and all his family. Never minimize the importance of declaring the gospel.

Read Romans 10:14

- What does this verse have to do with our devotional for today?
- Have you ever declared the gospel to someone? If so, how did it go?
- If you are a believer, who declared the gospel to you?

Prayer
Father, thank you that you have given us the distinct privilege of declaring your truth to our neighbors and to the nations who have yet to hear. May our voices

never be silenced. Would you draw more and more people to yourself so that this message would continue to move forward in our world today? We know that is your will, and we can trust you to do it. In Jesus' name we pray. Amen.

DAY 4

The baptism of the Holy Spirit

[11:15] "As I began to speak, the Holy Spirit fell on them just as on us at the beginning. [16] And I remembered the word of the Lord, how he said, 'John baptized with water, but you will be baptized with the Holy Spirit.'"

Baptism is a very important symbol in the Christian life. It is one of the main ways that we publicly identify ourselves as Christians. We are symbolically buried with Jesus in his death, meaning we are dead to sin and its power over us. Further, we are raised to newness of life. Just as Jesus was risen from the dead so we are risen to a new way of life (i.e., righteousness) and freed from the old way of life (i.e., sin). Baptism is truly symbolic of Christians being a new creation in Christ.

But in today's text, Peter recalls what Jesus said: when his Spirit comes, believers would be "baptized" in the Holy Spirit. This simply means that Christians would receive the Holy Spirit when they repented of their sin and followed him. Jesus calls the Holy Spirit the "Helper" who would dwell with you and be in you (John 14:16–17).

This is the promise of the New Covenant. In the Old Testament, or Old Covenant, God's Spirit was active, though in a different way: he indwelled the temple and his symbolic presence was found there. God's Spirit temporarily came upon different people in different ways for different tasks.

This doesn't seem to be the same permanent indwelling that we have in the New Covenant. We should be so thankful that we live in such a time as this, when we have access to the Holy Spirit. He dwells in us and gives us new desires to want to follow God. This is truly a blessing.

Read Romans 8:11

- How does Jesus dwell in us?
- What is the difference between how the Spirit worked in the Old Testament and the New Testament?
- How can you see the Spirit's work in your life?

Prayer

Father, thank you for giving us the Holy Spirit, along with new desires to follow you. Help us to stay in step with the Spirit. May you produce the fruit of your Spirit through our lives so that you may be glorified, and many are drawn to your love. In Jesus' name we pray. Amen.

DAY 5

You can't stand in God's way

[11:17] "If then God gave the same gift to them as he gave to us when we believed in the Lord Jesus Christ, who was I that I could stand in God's way?" [18] When they heard these things they fell silent. And they glorified God, saying, "Then to the Gentiles also God has granted repentance that leads to life."

Ever had a heated disagreement with someone? Perhaps there was a back-and-forth exchange of words over a few hours, with neither person willing to change their opinion—that is, until suddenly it dawned on you that you'd been wrong the whole time. All of a sudden, you saw things from a different perspective and knew that you should have spoken differently.

If you were to find yourselves in such a position, how do you think you would respond?

For many people, the response would probably be to fall silent. You see that the words you used before were wrong, and so a proper response might be to stop using words all together.

This happened to a guy named Job. He suffered greatly and, in response, pressed God over and over for answers to questions that God would not give him. Instead, God showed him how his mind could not handle the answers that he was seeking. So what did Job do? The Bible says that he put his hand over his mouth and pledged to speak no more (Job 40:4–5).

We also see this happening in today's text. Before being corrected by Peter, a group of Jewish leaders insisted that new Gentile Christian converts become Jewish first and practice their faith according to Jewish tradition. Upon learning of their misguided advice, they "fell silent" and from then on spoke only words of affirmation about God's plan.

Sometimes it is very wise to stop talking. One of those times is definitely when your words are counter to the plan of God.

Read Job 42:2

- How is this verse related to today's text?
- Have you ever resisted God's will?
- When is it wise to stop talking?

Prayer

Father, may you humble us like the people in these verses if we ever get in the way of your plan. May you close our mouths and help us to see by the power of your Spirit that your way is the best way. In love, resist us if we resist you. Help us to be humble. In Jesus' name we pray. Amen.

WEEK 11

Acts 11:19–30

DAY 1

A unique calling

[11:19] Now those who were scattered because of the persecution that arose over Stephen traveled as far as Phoenicia and Cyprus and Antioch, speaking the word to no one except Jews.

Are all people the same? If you have a brother or a sister, look at them. It would be safe to assume that you have much in common—e.g., same parents, same house, same last name, etc.—but are you completely the same?

Of course not. Even if you were identical twins, you wouldn't be exactly alike. No two people are.

This point has implications for how God uses people in the church. While we are part of the same family of God and have much in common—e.g., collectively loving God's mission, repenting regularly, and giving financially to make sure that the church continues—our specific callings can be very different.

As we have learned, God's plan was not just for Jewish people but for the whole world. So it makes sense that God would equip individuals to know how best to evangelize to others within their tradition.

Everyone has a different calling, and as we seek to support one another with our unique gifts, the church will become a place of beautiful togetherness.

Read 1 Corinthians 12:14–19

- What is your unique calling?
- If you don't know right now, what do you think it could be in the future?

Prayer

Father, thank you that you have not made us all the same but have given unique gifts to the body of Christ. May we glorify you in all our different ministries and callings. In Jesus' name we pray. Amen.

DAY 2

Suffering can lead to blessing

> [11:19] Now those who were scattered because of the persecution that arose over Stephen traveled as far as Phoenicia and Cyprus and Antioch, speaking the word to no one except Jews. [20] But there were some of them, men of Cyprus and Cyrene, who on coming to Antioch spoke to the Hellenists also, preaching the Lord Jesus. [21] And the hand of the Lord was with them, and a great number who believed turned to the Lord.

Sometimes persecution is a blessing. This doesn't mean that we should rejoice in evil. Evil is evil, and we should never glamorize it. But sometimes, God works in mysterious ways and uses things that are evil to bring about good.

The best example of this would be the cross of Jesus. What could possibly be more evil than murdering an innocent man in the most horrific way possible, let alone the Son of God? This was the pinnacle of evil on display. Yet, didn't God use this to bring about the most amazing news in all of history—sinners are pardoned and receive a heavenly inheritance that is glorious beyond comprehension? That is great news!

We also learn that the church was seriously persecuted after Stephen was stoned to death. But as a result, the followers of Jesus spread out to different places around the known world and the message of salvation grew and grew. This wouldn't have happened had not the believers been scattered first.

Suffering can lead to true blessing.

Read Romans 8:18

- What does this verse say about suffering?
- Why won't our suffering be worth comparing to what awaits us?
- In your life, have you ever seen suffering produce a future blessing?

Prayer

Father, thank you that you use the horrors that are perpetrated by evil men to glorify yourself and bless your people. May you help us to hold fast in faith when we are persecuted. Comfort us by the power of your Spirit. In Jesus' name we pray. Amen.

DAY 3

Full of the Holy Spirit and faith

[11:22] The report of this came to the ears of the church in Jerusalem, and they sent Barnabas to Antioch. [23] When he came and saw the grace of God, he was glad, and he exhorted them all to remain faithful to the Lord with steadfast purpose, [24] for he was a good man, full of the Holy Spirit and of faith. And a great many people were added to the Lord.

What are the personality attributes of the people you love? Do you love people who are selfless? Do you love people who are giving? Do you love people who are good listeners? How about people who are loyal and kind?

What kinds of people are truly a blessing to you?

In today's text, we learn that God loves to use certain kinds of people. We learn that Barnabas was sent to the church in Antioch to see for himself what was being reported about these people, along with a great number of Gentiles who were coming to faith.

Did you notice how Barnabas is described in these verses? It says that he was "full of the Holy Spirit" and "faith." These are the traits of the kind of people God loves to use. He usually doesn't use people who show no fruit and are faithless.

The good news is that God loves to give the Holy Spirit and faith to those who ask him. He is a loving Father who gives good gifts to his children.

Read Luke 11:11–13

- What do we learn about God's character in these verses?
- Would you like to ask God for more of the Holy Spirit?

Prayer

Father, thank you that you use those who are submitted to you and are willing to receive your Holy Spirit by faith. Thank you that you promise to give yourself to us when we ask. We are so needy. Please fill us more and more. In Jesus' name we pray. Amen.

DAY 4

Discipleship takes time

[11:25] So Barnabas went to Tarsus to look for Saul, [26] and when he had found him, he brought him to Antioch. For a whole year they met with the church and taught a great many people. And in Antioch the disciples were first called Christians.

Creating something beautiful usually takes quite a bit of time. If you are painting a picture of a stunning landscape or flower, it would probably take you more than five minutes to capture its beauty. Preparing an exquisite meal for a neighborhood party would probably take some time—you couldn't just whip that up in a jiffy. Building a beautiful church with majestic columns and high ceilings doesn't happen overnight. Beauty takes time to create.

The same is true of Christian discipleship. We learn in today's text that these new believers in Antioch needed to be discipled. So Barnabas got one of God's main teachers, the recently converted Saul, and brought him to this church. Did the text say that Saul stayed for only a day or two? No, it says that he stayed for a whole year teaching many different people how to truly follow Jesus.

This is a great reminder for us. Helping people follow Jesus takes time, which implies that we need to be filled with patience. This is one of the fruits of the Spirit (Gal. 5:22). Most people don't learn overnight how to surrender their lives to God's mission, how to repent, or how to reconcile with their enemies. We need to be taught, reminded, and given room in our lives to practice godliness.

Read Colossians 1:28–29

- Do you think the kind of maturity that Paul had in mind here was something that happened quickly?
- According to Paul, helping to disciple people requires strength. But whose strength is it?

Prayer

Father, help us to be patient. We need your patience flowing through us. May you use us to help more and more people grow in the grace and knowledge of our Lord Jesus. In Jesus' name we pray. Amen.

DAY 5

God's people take care of each other

[11:27] Now in these days prophets came down from Jerusalem to Antioch. [28] And one of them named Agabus stood up and fore-told by the Spirit that there would be a great famine over all the world (this took place in the days of Claudius). [29] So the disciples determined, every one according to his ability, to send relief to the brothers living in Judea. [30] And they did so, sending it to the elders by the hand of Barnabas and Saul.

One of the ways that Christians demonstrate that they love Jesus is by taking really good care of one another. What would you think of an organization that looked the other way when its members were in need of help? Or had members stealing from one another? Or made a habit out of putting one another down?

You'd probably want to steer clear of that organization, right?

God commands his people to take really good care of one another. This serves multiple purposes. First, it strengthens bonds in our churches. Second, it adds to the church's longevity. Third, it shows unbelievers what we believe, providing a great opportunity for evangelism. When people are converted and join the church, it encourages the whole organization.

In today's text, a prophet foretold of a worldwide famine that would threaten the church's progress. It came to pass, but Christians were faithful to take good care of one another, and the church was strengthened.

Read Galatians 6:10

- Who is someone in your church that you could serve in a tangible way?
- How might this action strengthen the church?

Prayer
Father, may we have a heart that seeks to serve and not be served. May that be our primary motivation. Fill us with your Spirit so that we can strengthen your church for your name's sake. In Jesus' name we pray. Amen.

SMALL GROUP STUDY

WEEK 1

Read Acts 6:1–7

Like pressure applied to levees during a flood, the early church experienced significant hindrances to its progress early on. The faithful proclamation of the gospel added many to the church; however, the resulting strain was so great that an entire group of widows "were being neglected in the daily distribution" of food, clothing, and financial resources (Acts 6:1), which, in turn, placed limitations on the preaching of the Word of God (Acts 6:2). These circumstances forced the leadership to make a decision: would they ignore the trouble, provide a Band-Aid solution, or try to get to the heart of the matter?

Not only were they able to resolve an issue that could have led to division, but by identifying the problem and being part of the solution, they set an example for future generations to follow (Acts 6:3, 5). The leaders learned to adapt: they removed the administrative burden from the apostles, which created an environment in which they could devote themselves to prayer and preaching (Acts 6:3–6).

God honored the church's decision: "And the word of God continued to increase, the number of the disciples multiplied greatly in Jerusalem, and a great many of the priests became obedient to the faith" (Acts 6:7).

Questions

- Why was caring for widows so important for the early church? (See Exodus 22:22; Deuteronomy 14:29, 16:11; and James 1:27.)
- How did church leadership and the church body respond to this situation? What can we learn from their example?
- What does this passage teach us about church leadership? How can we best support those called to "prayer and the ministry of the word"?
- Do you consider yourself someone who is enabling or disabling the church's mission? How are you currently serving your local church?

SMALL GROUP STUDY

WEEK 2

Read Acts 6:8–8:3

"The Times They Are a-Changin'"—this is the title of one of folksinger Bob Dylan's most famous songs. In penning these words, Dylan identified with the social turmoil that existed at that time in the United States. This song has enjoyed a lasting legacy by capturing one of the constant realities of our life and world: change.

Change is exactly what has happened to Christianity in Western civilization. Christianity is no longer the dominant worldview in our culture, and identifying yourself as a Christian will not earn you a lot of social benefits. If anything, professing faith in Jesus may lead your peers to mock, jeer, or ostracize you.

Persecution in any form should not come as a surprise. Jesus was persecuted, and we should expect the same—in varying degrees—if we strive to live and love like him (John 15:18–19; cf. 2 Tim. 3:12). So the question is not *if* we will experience persecution but *when*. When it does occur, we can follow the example of Stephen, the subject of this week's passage.

Stephen was considered to be a man "full of grace and power" who "was doing great wonders and signs among the people" (Acts 6:8). For proclaiming the gospel of Jesus Christ, he was disputed and lied about (Acts 6:9–15). Stephen didn't stoop to their level. His response was not the result of will-power and determination but rather the grace of God and the empowering presence of the Spirit (Acts 6:8). He didn't twist or change the message of the Bible but rather humbly, boldly, and graciously continued to proclaim its message.

Questions

- Stephen was falsely charged by the Jewish leaders, who claimed he said that Jesus would destroy the temple and change the customs of Moses (Acts 6:14). What was the significance of worshiping God at the temple? Why would worshiping at the temple no longer be necessary? (Read John 4:16–26.)

- Jesus said, "If the world hates you, know that it has hated me before it hated you" (John 15:18). Regardless of how great or small, have you experienced any level of persecution? What can we learn from Stephen's example when facing persecution?

- How did the church respond to Stephen's martyrdom and the persecution that ensued?

WEEK 3

Read Acts 8:4–25

Life doesn't always turn out the way we think it should. All of us will experience some level of pain, loss, and tragedy. In the moment, such experiences can be crushing, if not devastating. We can become consumed by these moments of grief and despair, and succumb to their burdens to the point that we turn in on ourselves, not out to God.

Regardless of our circumstance and situation, God has a way of working things out for his eternal good. He's promised to those who love him that he will "work all things together for good" (Rom. 8:28). We might not be able to see how God will take a tragedy in our life and work it out for our good and his glory, but thankfully he has provided us with many examples from the Scriptures, in particular Acts 8:4–25.

In last week's passage, we observed the martyrdom of Stephen followed by "a great persecution against the church" (Acts 8:1). This wave of oppression came like a mighty wind that scattered the church throughout the region. Despite being persecuted and displaced from their homes, those who were scattered didn't falter in their faith in God but "went about preaching the word" (Acts 8:4). What appears to the eye as a terrible situation was an event God orchestrated to further the spread of the gospel of Jesus beyond the confines of Jerusalem (cf. Gen. 50:20).

By the grace of God, look beyond the limitations of your struggles and fix your eyes on the God of hope who will complete the good work in your life he began (Phil. 1:6).

Questions

- What motivated Philip to travel to Samaria? (Read Acts 8:4.)
- The Samaritans were ostracized from the Jewish population, yet this was the first group of people outside the Jewish community to receive

the gospel. What does this tell us about the mercy, grace, and intent of God in building his church?

- Simon attempted to manipulate God for his own personal desires (Acts 8:18–19). Do you attempt to manipulate or bargain with him?

WEEK 4

Read Acts 8:26–40

Jesus is alive, and he is building his church (Matt. 16:18). Changes in the culture do not concern him, Satan cannot stop him, and the church's apathy will not slow him down. As a general who leads his troops, Jesus is calling, leading, and mobilizing us through the presence and power of the Holy Spirit to participate in his work. This is exactly what we observe in this week's passage.

In Acts 8:1–5, we followed Philip as he left Jerusalem and travelled throughout Judea and Samaria where he proclaimed the gospel of Jesus Christ. God blessed his efforts by performing signs and wonders through him, drawing a crowd and saving many of them. The church continued to grow beyond these regions through the urging of the Spirit of God and Philip's faithful obedience. From leading Philip to Gaza (Acts 8:26) to physically teleporting him to another town like a Star Trek teleporter, the Holy Spirit took initiative in leading Philip.

When placing our faith in Christ, God does not hand us a copy of the Bible and tell us to figure things out. This isn't the case at all. After calling us and giving us new life, the Holy Spirit takes up residence in our lives. He indwells and fills us with his presence (John 14:17; Eph. 5:18). He guides us (Ps. 23:2), sanctifies us (1 Cor. 6:11), and empowers us to be a witness for Jesus (Acts 1:8).

God the Holy Spirit is at work in the world, our lives, and the church. He is mediating the presence of Jesus Christ in our lives and in the church through his marvelous gospel.

Questions

- The Holy Spirit takes a personal and active role leading Philip (Acts 8:26, 29, 39) as well as our individual lives (Rom. 8:4; Gal. 5:16). Are you aware of the Holy Spirit's guidance in your life? How do you sense his guidance day to day?

- As the Holy Spirit led Philip to witness to the Ethiopian eunuch, he will lead us, too, to share Jesus with others. Who in your life do you believe the Holy Spirit is leading you to share Jesus with? How are you trusting God to empower you to share Jesus (Acts 1:8)?
- God pursued the unnamed Ethiopian through Philip. How has God pursued you? Did he work through certain people or events in order to lead you to him?

WEEK 5

Read Acts 9:1–9

In life we will meet people, have experiences, and even read books that will influence who we are, what we do, or what we think. Sometimes these changes are rapid; at other times, they're slow and ongoing. Unlike the caterpillar's metamorphosis into a butterfly, which takes time, when we place our faith in Jesus for the forgiveness of our sin, we are transformed into a new creation immediately (2 Cor. 5:17). We are given a new life, new desires, and a new eternal destination. This radical transformation we experience in Christ is powerfully exemplified in Saul's encounter with Jesus.

Saul was filled with an insatiable anger that drove him to persecute the church. He sought and received authority to arrest those "he found . . . belonging to the Way" (Acts 9:1–2). Traveling to Damascus in search of Christians to arrest and extradite, Saul encountered Jesus Christ. Relating this encounter, Luke writes, "A light from heaven flashed around him" (Acts 9:3). This great light stopped Saul in his tracks and brought him to the ground. Jesus not only asked Saul why he was persecuting him, but he called him to rise from the ground, enter the city, and meet a man who would tell him what to do next (Acts 9:4–5). Upon rising to his knees, Saul discovered that the light had blinded him, requiring his companions to escort him to the city (Acts 9:6–9).

Saul's encounter with Jesus would forever change his life and our world. While our individual encounters with Jesus may not be as radical as Saul's, his life does exemplify what can occur in our life and in the church.

Questions

- This week may be a good time for the group to share their salvation experiences. From past experiences and influences to God's present-day work in each one's life, how has each member of the group encountered Jesus and seen God at work?

- Regardless of whether we think someone is beyond the reach of God's mercy and grace, Saul's experience proves otherwise. God can soften the hardest of hearts. Is there anyone in your life that you've given up on meeting Jesus? Identify 1–3 people in your life you can pray for and share the gospel with.

WEEK 6

Read Acts 9:10–19a

No one is beyond the reach of God's mercy and grace. God is not limited by the sins we've committed, our opposition to the gospel, or how old we are. He is more than able to change our life in Christ. Sometimes we as the church are reluctant to reach out to those beyond the comfort of our four walls or even accept those with a checkered past as brothers and sisters in Christ. But in this week's passage, we observe a great example of how Christians can accept those outside the faith in addition to the church's role in discipling believers.

Ananias makes a cameo appearance in the book of Acts here and elsewhere. While in Damascus, the Lord appeared to him in a vision and asked him to "lay his hands on [Saul] so that he might regain his sight" (Acts 9:2). In response, Ananias rightfully expressed concerns because Saul had been laying hands on Christians, not to pray for them but to arrest them (Acts 9:13–14). God confirms his request and clarifies for Ananias that Saul is his chosen instrument to share the gospel with the "Gentiles and kings and the children of Israel" (Acts 9:15). As an expression of faith and trust in God, Ananias went to Saul, prayed for him, and God fulfilled his promise by giving Saul his vision back.

All of us can sympathize with Ananias and why he was reluctant to approach Saul—he was a persecutor of Christians. Though many of us will never wrestle with the tension created by welcoming into the body of Christ a former persecutor of the church, most of us will wrestle with welcoming new believers into the church. They act, speak, and dress differently from those of us who have matured in Christ for years. But like Ananias and the early church, we too need to be prepared to embrace those new to the faith and recognize God's power to save and transform even those most opposed to him. Although our faith in Jesus is an individual decision, we as the church play an important role in reaching and discipling people.

Questions

- Do you relate more to the struggles of Paul, the fresh face establishing himself in the church community, or Ananias, the seasoned believer wary of newcomers? Is there anyone in your life God is prompting you to connect with that you have reservations about?

- Think of a time when you didn't immediately obey God. Why did you hesitate? Now, think of a time when you immediately obeyed God with something difficult. How was this experience different?

- Through prayer, God molds our will into his own. We see this exemplified in Ananias' conversation with God in this week's passage. Do you consider prayer in this way? Do you talk with God about your struggles?

- Like Ananias, we play an important role in the spiritual maturation of other Christians. Has God placed anyone in your life you can reach out to like Ananias did with Saul?

SMALL GROUP STUDY

WEEK 7

Read Acts 9:19b–31

Saul lived uncomfortably in the middle. He was reluctantly accepted by the church—twice (Acts 9:13–14, 26). And his preaching ministry placed him on the Jews' and Greeks' most-wanted list (Acts 9:23, 29). This week's passage gives us a look into the life of Saul and how he lived life between these polarizing groups.

Saul was caught in a chaotic cycle of rinse and repeat. Soon after regaining his sight and strength (Acts 9:18–19), he began proclaiming the gospel in synagogues (Acts 9:20). Many, including the synagogue, were less than impressed—they plotted to kill him (Acts 9:23–24). From here, Saul escaped the city, traveled to Jerusalem, and went through the experience yet again.

Many will have experiences similar to Saul's when coming to faith in Jesus. People you used to associate with may no longer accept you and you may find it difficult finding community within the church. Thankfully our relationship with God is not based on the faithfulness of others toward us but rather Jesus' faithfulness toward us. Remarks the author of Hebrews,

> "Therefore, since we are surrounded by so great a cloud of witnesses, let us also lay aside every weight, and sin which clings so closely, and let us run with endurance the race that is set before us, looking to Jesus, the founder and perfecter of our faith, who for the joy that was set before him endured the cross, despising the shame, and is seated at the right hand of the throne of God" (Heb. 12:1–2).

Questions

- Can you relate to Saul's (Paul) experience of living uncomfortably in the middle?

- What was your experience like when you devoted your life to Jesus? How did your family and friends respond to your decision? Did you have an easy or difficult time finding community in church?
- Paul and countless others throughout history provide encouraging examples of a life lived wholeheartedly for Jesus. How can we find encouragement from Paul's example of faith?

WEEK 8

Read Acts 9:32–43

"The time is fulfilled, and the kingdom of God is at hand," declared Jesus (Mark 1:15). God's kingdom represents his rule and reign on earth, especially in the hearts of men and women (John 18:36). The book of Acts captures the inauguration of the kingdom of God and its rapid advancement through the preaching of the gospel (Acts 1–2).

Luke now transitions from highlighting God's work in and through Paul and turns the spotlight back to Peter. This week's passage not only serves as a transition in his historical accounts, but it also sets the stage for the next great advancement of the gospel to the Gentiles in Acts 11–12.

We catch back up with Peter as he's visiting people during his travels. While in a town called Lydda, Peter comes across a paralyzed man by the name of Aeneas, whom God heals in Jesus' name. We are told that all the residents of Lydda and Sharon, upon seeing Aeneas healed, "turned to the Lord" (Acts 9:32–35).

Soon after, Peter was asked by disciples of a neighboring town to accompany them to Joppa. He was taken to an upper room of a house where a girl named Tabitha lay dead. Peter commanded her to rise. Stories of her resurrection spread throughout the town, and many believed in the Lord (Acts 9:36–42).

These miraculous occurrences didn't happen at a stadium event with bright lights, a singing choir, or thumping bass. God miraculously healed Aeneas and Tabitha through Peter (Heb. 2:1–4). These miraculous occurrences didn't take place to make Peter famous; these events were meant to bring glory to God and lead people to faith in Jesus Christ.

Let them remind us of God's miraculous work in our own lives, graciously saving us in Christ, leading us in his wisdom, and answering prayers. Let us be quick to turn attention away from ourselves to Christ.

Questions

- Do you think Aeneas or Tabitha did anything before dying that encouraged God to heal them? What do we learn about God, grace, and faith from their examples?
- Like Aeneas and Tabitha, have you experienced God's power when you were helpless? If so, how?
- How are you trusting in God's power today? Do you need prayer for God to do something you can't do on your own?

WEEK 9

Read Acts 10:1–48

"We must face the sad fact that at eleven o'clock on Sunday morning," began Martin Luther King, Jr., "when we stand to sing 'In Christ there is no East or West,' we stand in the most segregated hour of America."[1] These words do more than paint a picture of the modern national landscape of the church; they reflect the kinds of barriers that existed in the early church before God intervened.

Acts 10 records an amazing time and transition in the life of the early church. God orchestrated the demolition of the dividing wall between Jews and Gentiles by ordaining Peter to meet with Cornelius and to share with him and those present with him these words: "To [Jesus] all the prophets bear witness that everyone who believes in him receives forgiveness of sins through his name" (Acts 10:43). God confirmed his acceptance of the Gentiles by visibly pouring out his Spirit on them as he had done previously for the Jews (Acts 10:46; cf. Acts 2:1–4).

God does not show favoritism to any one person or group (Acts 10:34). All men and women have been created in his image and the projected walls that may separate us socially have no room in the church. In Christ, we are all brothers and sisters. Our race, ethnicity, or bank account is not the common denominator for social acceptance in the church—Jesus is.

Questions

- God dramatically displayed his acceptance of the Gentiles. What does this event in church history mean for us today?

- This event reveals that God accepts all of us based on what his Son has done for us. Do you struggle with accepting certain people groups? Are there certain behaviors, appearances, or customs that

[1] Martin Luther King Jr., "Remaining Awake through a Great Revolution" (sermon, National Cathedral, Washington, DC, March 31, 1968).

cause you to distance yourself from people? If so, how do you think this compares to God's acceptance of us through Christ?

- Is your relationship with God up one day and down the next? Do your actions influence how you think God feels about you? How does this event encourage you to understand that God's relationship with us is based on the works of Jesus?

WEEK 10

Read Acts 11:1–18

Criticism is a close companion of creativity. Whether you're creating a new idea, a paper for class, or even a new ministry in the church, the presence of criticism is not far behind. Whether it's merited or not, there are many sources of criticism, especially those that express the fear of something new and different. This is exactly what Peter faced back in Jerusalem.

After God extended the gospel to the Gentiles and smashed the social barriers that existed between them and the Jews, the "circumcision party" in Jerusalem criticized Peter and his recent exploits (Acts 11:2). We're not told why they had a problem, but whatever it was, it was clear they didn't like Peter's association with the Gentiles.

We can learn a great deal from Peter's response to the criticism he received. He didn't become angry and vengeful. He didn't cower in submission and hide in the corner. And he didn't seek to minimize or belittle their opinion. He simply recounted the events and brought glory to God. In doing so, his audience was won over. What could have been a divisive time in the church turned out to be a unifying moment.

Questions

- Why did the "circumcision party" criticize Peter? How is their criticism similar to the criticism we level against other people or churches for conducting "new" ministries?

- Peter saw God's desire to include the Gentiles, so he stepped out of God's way (Acts 11:17). Is there any work of God in your life, family, or church that you're standing in the way of? If so, why?

- How do you handle criticism? Do you tend to react negatively or respond openly? What can you learn from Peter's example?

WEEK 11

Read Acts 11:19–30

The church wasn't going to be the same. The gospel of Jesus Christ was breaking new ground in dramatic ways. Acts 10:9–11:18 marks a cataclysmic shift in the life of the church. God was pouring out his Spirit on the Gentiles and ushering them into his family for the first time through faith in Jesus Christ. Our passage this week captures the first efforts in directly reaching out to this new group of people.

The persecution that followed the martyrdom of Stephen led many people to travel far and wide, and along their journey to new lands and cities, these unnamed faithful followers of Jesus continued to predominantly share the gospel with the Jews (Acts 11:19). "There were some," records Luke, "who on coming to Antioch spoke to the Hellenists also, preaching the Lord Jesus" (Acts 11:20). The Lord blessed their efforts, and many repented of their sin and turned in faith to Jesus Christ.

The names of the "some" are not recorded. We may never know who they are, but this may be exactly the point. This event can be easily passed over when reading, but this moment captured by Luke is of extreme importance in the life of the church because it marks the first direct outreach to the Gentiles. God did not send in the "big guns" like Peter and Paul; he carried out his work for his glory through "some" people. "Some" people throughout history are primarily responsible for "most" of the church growth. "Some" people each and every single day choose whether or not to tell their family, friends, and neighbors about Jesus. Look beyond your status, gifts, and abilities to God who will empower you to be a witness (Acts 1:8).

Questions

- An unnamed group declared the gospel of Jesus Christ and a "great number" of people turned to faith in him. Does their example and God's faithfulness encourage you to share your faith?

SMALL GROUP STUDY

- When it comes to sharing our faith, we tend to gravitate toward opposite ends of the spectrum: self-reliance or God-reliance. Which do you find yourself gravitating toward? In this passage, the unnamed group shared their faith, and God blessed their efforts. Do you share your faith with others?

- In response to the message delivered by Agabus, the disciples provided relief for Christians in Judea based on their ability. Is there anyone in your life or the group's who needs financial relief? This could be an opportune time to identify someone to love and support.

GROUP INDUCTIVE STUDY

WEEK 1

Read Acts 6:1–7

Introduction

For some, change is uncomfortable. Think of a time when your church changed—leaders did something you disagreed with, or needs went unfulfilled. How did you react? Did you bring up the issue to leaders? Did you pray about it? Perhaps you felt a bit disgruntled?

The church is full of people who are at different places in their walk with Jesus. In a growing church, current systems adapt to address needs. Yet we may become critical when we don't like the music, the sermon, the new time for Bible study, or the leadership style. These issues arise because people have different desires, expectations, and ideas.

Sadly, conflict often threatens to derail or overshadow the gospel proclamation, which is Jesus' primary mission for the church. In Acts, the main job of the apostles was to testify about Jesus. The church's one overarching goal was to spread the gospel in order to make disciples. As members of the same church, it ought to be our main goal, too.

Observation

The Jerusalem church was a microcosm of the diverse city.[2] Until now, the Christian community was bound to Judaism and the temple, and Hebrew Christians likely spoke Aramaic. However, the growth of the church resulted in the creation of new communities, and within each, widows were economically and socially vulnerable, having no family or property.

- In Acts 6:1, what dispute arises? Why was this an issue? Read Acts 4:34–35. See also Exodus 22:22, and Deuteronomy 14:29, 16:11, 14, and 24:19 as examples of caring for widows.

[2] Ajith Fernando, *Acts*, NIVAC (Grand Rapids: Zondervan, 1998), 228–30.

111

- How did the apostles respond, and what instructions were given to solve the problem?
- How did the church body respond to the apostles' instructions?
- Describe the character of those chosen to help the widows.
- What did the apostles do to show they approved of these men?
- What was the result of resolving this dispute?

Interpretation

When disputes arise in the church, we often can't see beyond the situation at hand. However, church issues arise while we're spreading the gospel, making disciples, and bringing about God's kingdom. This dispute between the Hellenists and the Hebrews was the devil's third attack, intended to derail the spread of the gospel.[3] As we will see, the devil had already tried corruption and persecution. This time, he tried distraction. He was trying to preoccupy the apostles with performing administrative tasks rather than preaching the Word.

- What were Jesus' instructions to the apostles before ascending back into heaven? Read Acts 1:8 and Matthew 28:18–20. Why were the apostles especially appointed to begin the spread of the gospel? Read Acts 1:21–22.
- What growth had the church previously experienced? See Acts 1:15; 2:41, 47; 4:4; 5:14. What threats had the church experienced? See Acts 5:1–11 and 5:17–18. How does the dispute in Acts 6:1–7 differ?
- How do we know that the church body respected the apostles' leadership?
- When the church quickly and cooperatively handles internal disputes, resulting in good relationships and assistance, what does this communicate to the culture around us? What message does the church send if it is divided or does not resolve disputes lovingly?

[3] John R. W. Stott, *The Message of Acts*, BST (Downers Grove, IL: IVP, 1990), 120.

Application

Churches should lead people to Christ, disciple them well, mature them in character, and raise them up to lead the church.[4] Let us think both about the church's mission in the world and our individual part in it.

- What distracts you from supporting the church's mission of spreading the gospel? Does this need to be addressed with a leader, do you need to pray about it, or do you need to let the cause of distraction go for the sake of the gospel?

- What does Acts 6 teach us about roles in the local church? What should pastors and elders be focused on? What roles can deacons, other leaders, and members fulfill to assist pastors, just like "the seven" did for the apostles?

- How are you currently serving your local church? How conscious are you of the universal church—that is, the progress of the gospel in other countries? In what other ways could you serve the church locally or globally—including serving practically, giving money, praying, or other means?

For Further Study

- "Serving Widows, Preaching the Word, and Winning Priests" by John Piper, http://www.desiringgod.org/sermons/serving-widows-preaching-the-word-and-winning-priests
- "Service in Christ" by Leo Schuster, http://sermons.redeemer.com/store/index.cfm?fuseaction=product.display&product_ID=19790&ParentCat=6
- "3 Leadership Lessons from Acts 6" by Joe Stengele, http://theresurgence.com/2013/11/23/3-leadership-lessons-from-acts-6

---

[4] Joe Stengele, "3 Leadership Lessons from Acts 6," *The Resurgence* (blog), http://theresurgence.com/2013/11/23/3-leadership-lessons-from-acts-6.

WEEK 2

Read Acts 6:8–8:3

Introduction

Zealous preacher William Jenkyn was jailed at age seventy-two for refusing to stop preaching after being labeled a nonconformist by England's royal court. Physicians warned King James II that Jenkyn's life was in danger and petitioned for his release, to which the King responded, "Jenkyn shall be a prisoner as long as he lives." After Jenkyn's death, a nobleman informed the king that the prisoner was free; when the King asked who had done this, the nobleman replied, "A King greater than your Majesty—the King of kings."[5]

Throughout Christian history, there have been countless men and women like William Jenkyn who, despite persecution and death threats, continued to preach the gospel. What enables some to witness so courageously? Jesus said, "You will receive power when the Holy Spirit has come upon you, and you will be my witnesses in Jerusalem and in all Judea and Samaria, and to the end of the earth" (Acts 1:8).

Acts 6 introduces us to Stephen, a Hellenistic Jewish-Christian convert appointed as a deacon to care for widows. As Stephen's witness for Jesus spread, a group of Hellenistic Jews from North Africa challenged him, accusing him of blasphemy before the Sanhedrin. Stephen, with his face shining like that of an angel, tore apart their revisionist history and false confidences before God (Acts 7:1–53).

The men of the Sanhedrin became enraged, but Stephen, unfazed, looked toward heaven and saw the glory of God! He declared, "Behold, I see the heavens opened and the Son of Man standing at the right hand of the Father" (Acts 7:56). Upon hearing Stephen's words, the crowd dragged him from the city and stoned him. Stephen fell to his knees, asked Jesus to show his killers mercy, and died, becoming the New Testament church's first martyr.

[5] Herbert Lockyer, *Last Words of Saints and Sinners* (Grand Rapids: Kregel, 1969), 206.

Just when we think this scene in God's story could not be any more dramatic, we meet Saul, who not only approved of Stephen's death, but also went on to ravage the church. But God used the very persecution meant to stop Jesus' disciples to scatter them, thus beginning the work of the Great Commission (Matt. 28:16–20), thrusting them into the very places Jesus commanded them to go.

Observation

- What evidence is given for Stephen's ability to serve the church and preach the gospel?

- Read Acts 7:2–35. Where was Abraham living when God made his covenant promise? What country was Joseph living in when God used him to rescue the Israelites? Where were the Israelites when God sent Moses to deliver them? How would these examples of God's presence outside the temple, and his rescuing work outside the Holy Land, have challenged the Jewish council's understanding of their purposes?

- Read John 2:20–22. Why would worshiping at the temple no longer be necessary?

- Stephen called the council "stiff-necked people, uncircumcised in heart and ears." Who does Stephen say they resist? Who does he accuse them of murdering?

- What was Saul's response to Stephen's trial? What was the effect of the persecution of the church?

Interpretation

- The Sanhedrin Council was the supreme Jewish court made up of high priests, elders, and scribes, all devoted to a complex system of rabbinic tradition, yet missing the clear evidence of God's presence. What evidence of God's presence was overlooked by the Sanhedrin in Acts 6:15?

- Hebrews 11:1 describes faith as "confidence in what we hope for and assurance about what we do not see." In Stephen's response, he emphasized Abraham's faith prior to knowing where he was going (7:3). Read John 14:6. Similarly, why would it require great faith for Jews to believe 'Jesus is the way'?

- "The sting of death is sin" because "the wages of sin is death." How does Christ's conquest of sin enable Stephen to face imminent death with such peace and effectually say, "Death, where's your sting?" How is the Holy Spirit revealed in his demeanor?

- Stephen's arrest, trial, and murder bears remarkable resemblance to Jesus' arrest, trial, and murder, including asking God to forgive his killers. How is Stephen's prayer answered in the life of Saul?

- When Stephen looked into heaven, he saw Jesus standing at the right hand of the Father, as if greatly moved by the suffering of his people. Read Psalm 116:15. How does God describe the death of his holy ones?

Application

- Stephen's point to the council is that it is possible to possess the land, the law, and the temple without having Christ himself. What places and practices do you rely on to feel God's presence? How is God calling you to rely, instead, on the indwelling of the Holy Spirit?

- The Jews prided themselves on being Abraham's descendants with a rich Jewish heritage. In what ways do you rely more on your Christian upbringing or knowledge than on faith in Jesus?

- Second Timothy 3:12 says that everyone who wants to live a godly life will be persecuted. How do you respond when you are persecuted for Christ's name? How does looking to eternity enable you to respond with patience and joy?

- When suffering, do you doubt Jesus' nearness? What things do you turn to for comfort rather than relying on the Comforter? What is the Holy Spirit asking you to confess?

For Further Study

- *Last Words of Sinners and Saints* by Herbert Lockyer
- *Acts* by John Calvin
- *Acts* by Kent Hughes
- "Death of a Spirit Filled Man" by John Piper, http://www.desiring-god.org/sermons/the-death-of-a-spirit-filled-man?lang=en
- "Angry Jesus Cleanses the Temple" by Mark Driscoll, http://marshill.com/media/luke/angry-jesus-cleanses-the-temple

WEEK 3

Read Acts 8:4–25

Introduction

Two thousand years out, it's easy to miss how shocking the salvation of the Samaritans would have been to the Jewish Christian community. The Samaritan people were neither Gentiles nor were they Jews; they were a detested third entity. The route from Jerusalem to Galilee was through the land of Samaria, but Orthodox Jews would take a much longer route, just to avoid being defiled by an "unclean" people. The Samaritans, in turn, despised the Jews, claiming the Pentateuch (the first five books of the Bible) as their own but changing words and sacred places to fit themselves.[6] In John 8:48, the Jews, seeking to slander Jesus, accuse him of having a demon and being a Samaritan.

And now we read how God scatters the young church into Judea and Samaria (Acts 8:1–4). The spread of the gospel beyond the boundaries of Jerusalem may seem inevitable from our point of view, but it took tragedy and subsequent persecution to disperse the believers across the region. John Stott explains, "What is plain is that the devil (who lurks behind all persecution of the church), overreached himself. His attack had the opposite effect to what he intended. Instead of smothering the gospel, persecution succeeded only in spreading it."[7]

Observation

- What circumstances brought Philip to Samaria? What did he say and do there? How did the Samaritan people respond?

---

[6] John B. Polhill, *Acts*, NAC (Nashville: Broadman, 1992), 214–15.

[7] John R. W. Stott, *The Spirit, the Church, and the World: The Message of Acts* (Wheaton, IL: IVP, 1990), 146.

- The Greek word *prosecho* is used three times in verses 4–13. It means "to pay close attention to something, give heed to, follow."[8] Find the verses in which this phrase is used and note what or whom the people are paying attention to as well as their responses.
- What did Simon say about himself? What name had the people of Samaria given him?
- Why did Peter and John travel to Samaria?
- What is Peter's interpretation (via the Holy Spirit) of Simon's heart?

Interpretation

To learn more about the origins of the Samaritan people, read 2 Kings 17:24–29, Ezra 4:1–5 (the "adversaries" described in this section are leaders from the province of Samaria), and John 4:7–24. The Samaritan religion went through many changes to become what it was in Jesus' day, but one thing remained: the animosity between the Jews and Samaritans, kindled through the centuries by mutual acts of violence and the Samaritans' eventual claim that they were the true chosen people of God.

- With so much hatred on either side, what does it tell you about God's grace and mercy that the Samaritans were the first people outside the main Jewish community to whom the gospel was preached?
- Luke uses the phrase "the word" (ESV) throughout this passage to describe the giving and receiving of the gospel. What is he trying to highlight about the gospel message? (See Romans 10:17 and John 17:14–17.)
- Verse 13 tells us even Simon himself believed and was baptized, yet in Peter's strong rebuke, he says Simon's heart is not right before God (v. 21). Is it possible to believe and not be saved? What is the

---

[8] Walter Bauer, et al., *A Greek-English Lexicon of the New Testament and Other Early Christian Literature*, 3rd ed. (Chicago: University of Chicago Press, 2001), 879–80.

difference between mere belief and saving faith? (See James 2:19; Romans 8:6–9, 10:9–10; and John 3:3–8.)

- In verses 15–17, we read about the coming of the Holy Spirit to the Samaritan believers. How is this a unique event?

- Read John 3:8, Ephesians 2:13–14, 18, and Romans 8:16. Why did God delay pouring out the Holy Spirit until the arrival of the apostles Peter and John?

- What does it mean to be in the gall of bitterness and bound by iniquity (v. 23)? How were these things motivating Simon?

Application

- The Jews regarded the Samaritan people with great contempt and hostility, viewing them as heretics and half-breeds. Is there a specific person or people group you've rejected sharing the gospel with? If so, why?

- The Greek word translated as "to pay attention to" implies a close attention, following, intentionally turning one's mind toward something. When the people of Samaria were closely following Simon, they were "amazed." When they turned this careful attention to Philip, there was "much joy." What do you spend your days paying attention to? In turn, how does what you pay attention to impact your thoughts and actions?

- Sorcery is an effort to manipulate, control, change, or redirect God.[9] Simon longed to manipulate and control the power of God for his own purpose and glory. In what ways do you make yourself believe you could harness the will and power of God for yourself?

- The Holy Spirit moved powerfully through Peter and John, bestowing gifts and speaking words of truth. When have you

[9] Mark Driscoll, "Will Man Rob God?" December 29, 2013, transcript, Mars Hill Church, http://marshill.com/media/malachi-living-for-a-legacy/will-man-rob-god.

encountered the power and direction of the Holy Spirit? How did you respond?

For Further Study

- "The Difference between Amazement and Faith" by Paul Tripp, http://marshill.com/media/best-sermon-ever/dr-paul-tripp-the-difference-between-amazement-and-faith-mark-6-45–52

WEEK 4

Read Acts 8:26–40

Introduction

Imagine during a Sunday worship service, a crazy thought enters your mind. You can't shake it. You need to leave church and walk to a nearby coffee shop. It's not that you lack focus on the sermon or you suddenly crave a chai latte; this is a direction not from your own imagination but from the Holy Spirit. As you enter the coffee shop, you notice an open seat next to an unusual-looking fellow. He's not dressed like most folks in this part of town. He's obviously not from around here. Perhaps even a foreigner. His head is buried deep in a book, and as he looks up with puzzlement on his face, he turns to you and asks, "I don't get this. What does John 3:16 mean anyway?"[10]

The Holy Spirit has set up the perfect opportunity for you to share the good news of Jesus Christ with a stranger.

In this section of Acts, we see the Holy Spirit call Philip from success in Samaria, where many convert, to a lonely desert road between Jerusalem and Gaza. Here, the story of the early church and the unfolding of God's salvation plan begin a new path. To this point, the good news of Jesus has been preached to crowds, and conversion has happened en mass. Now, we see how God uses Philip the Evangelist to save one man—and not any man but an Ethiopian eunuch, with dark skin, from a land far away, and physically maimed in such a way that even though he fears the Lord, he can never enter the temple courts to worship in his presence.

Luke's account demonstrates that God will position each of us to reveal his glory. The Ethiopian eunuch shows us that no matter our background, God will answer the questions of those who ask with a humble and sincere heart. And

---

[10] Adapted from K. O. Gangel, *Acts*, Holman New Testament Commentary (Nashville, TN: Broadman & Holman, 1998), 127. Accessed January 9, 2014, via Logos software.

most importantly, through the power of the Holy Spirit with the good news of Jesus Christ, God will radically save the unlikely.

Observation

- Who are the main characters in this passage, both physical and spiritual?
- Where was Philip previously (Acts 8:4–25), and what had he been doing? Why does he now change his location?
- Where was the Ethiopian returning from? What is a eunuch? What do we know about his social status in Ethiopia?
- What was the eunuch doing as Philip approached his chariot? Why is this important?
- How does Philip guide the eunuch? How does the eunuch respond? What action is taken to memorialize their encounter?
- Where do Philip and the eunuch go next (implied)?

Interpretation

- Read Jonah 1:1–3. How was Jonah called to Nineveh, and how did he respond? How was Philip called to the eunuch, and how did he respond? Who initiates salvation both in these accounts and in all situations? Using Jonah and Philip as examples, what part do we play in the story of salvation?
- Some scholars differ on whether the Ethiopian was a physical eunuch. If he had been one, how would Deuteronomy 23:1 have impacted his recent visit to Jerusalem? How did Philip's encounter with the eunuch fulfill Acts 1:8?
- The eunuch is reading from Isaiah 53:7–8, an Old Testament book that prophesies of the coming Messiah. The specific section fore-tells a Suffering Servant. Philip began with this Scripture (Acts 8:35) and told the good news of Jesus, although his actual words are not recorded. Using Acts 8:32–33, how do you think Philip specifically revealed Christ to the eunuch?

- What three questions does the eunuch ask Philip (vv. 31, 34, and 36)? What do these questions suggest about his character?
- Read Isaiah 56:3–8. Two barriers prevent the eunuch from being considered a "full Jew": his ethnicity and his physical mutilation. What is the answer to the eunuch's question in Acts 8:36?
- Philip has just previously proclaimed Christ in Samaria (8:4–8). Why was Simon the Magician not accepted by church leadership (vv. 20–24)? What do the baptism of the eunuch and the challenge to Simon reveal about what God values (v. 21)?

Application

- The Holy Spirit commands Philip to leave Samaria, a region where crowds come to Christ, and witness to one unlikely Ethiopian. God values one soul as much as a crowd, and often calls us to what the world deems foolish or unfruitful. How is the Holy Spirit calling you to an unlikely, seemingly unfruitful place?
- The Ethiopian eunuch is returning from Jerusalem, the city of Jesus' death and resurrection, now filled with several thousand Christian believers. Either he was oblivious that the Messiah had come or had rejected it, yet the Holy Spirit chases him down literally through the feet of Philip. How has God pursued you or is currently pursuing you in order to save you?
- What are some common barriers you construct that you mistakenly believe keep you from Christ? What promises from Scripture demolish those barriers? Make a list with your group members of the many barriers and promises that refute them to keep for future moments when the Holy Spirit directs you to share the good news of Jesus.

For Further Study

You may notice that the ESV omits Acts 8:37 as do most common translations. You can find Acts 8:37 in the KJV, NKJV, and NASB. Acts 8:37 (NKJV) reads as follows: "Then Philip said, 'If you believe with all your heart, you may.' And he answered and said, 'I believe that Jesus Christ is the Son of God.'"

Scholars believe that verse 37 was not original to Luke's account, as it does not occur in some of the earliest and most highly regarded versions of Acts. A copyist is believed to have added it at some point. John Polhill states,

> The added verse, however, has considerable value. It seems to embody a very early Christian baptismal confession where the one baptizing asked the candidate if he believed in Christ with all his heart, to which the candidate would respond by confessing Jesus Christ as the Son of God. This old confession is of real significance to the history of early Christian confessions and would be appropriate to the baptismal ceremony today.[11]

[11] John B. Polhill, *Acts*, NAC (Nashville: Broadman, 1992), 226.

WEEK 5

Read Acts 9:1–9

Introduction

Ever heard of a "come to Jesus" moment? Saul's story may be the most famous of all. With the blood of early Christians on his hands, and on his way to capture more victims of his religious rage, Saul meets the living God on a dusty desert road in Syria and is truly blinded by the light.

The scene opens amid a backdrop of tremendous persecution against the church, resulting in the scattering of believers throughout Judea and Samaria, and the ensuing spread of the gospel of Jesus. The opening line of the text reads "But Saul, still . . ."

Who is this Saul? Saul was a native of Tarsus, a tentmaker by trade, a citizen of Rome, of remarkable Jewish lineage as a member of the strictest religious sect called the Pharisees, boasting an impeccable adherence to the Jewish law. He received an excellent education under the tutelage of the great philosopher, Gamaliel (Acts 22:3) and was well acquainted with Greek philosophy and literature (Phil. 3:4–6).[12]

As we read the words "But Saul, still breathing threats and murder," we are catapulted back to the stoning of Stephen, the first martyr in the New Testament church, where Saul was present at and approved of Stephen's execution (Acts 7:58; 8:1–3). Even as Stephen was being laid to rest, Saul was "ravaging the church" by entering house after house and "dragging off men and women to prison."

In *The Christian Faith*, Michael Horton states, "Warfare is discovered especially whenever the progress of the gospel most threatens the kingdom of Satan,"[13] and in the midst of such warfare we find Saul of Tarsus, an

---

[12] Herbert Lockyer, *All the Men of the Bible* (Grand Rapids: Zondervan, 1958), 26.

[13] Michael Horton, *The Christian Faith: A Systematic Theology for Pilgrims on the Way* (Grand Rapids: Zondervan, 2011), 972–73.

instrumental agent in the persecution of the early church. Saul was a man full of fiery passion, steeped in religion and on a misguided mission to annihilate the church of Jesus.

Observation

- In verses 1 and 2, what was Saul's express intent and desire?
- Describe what happened as Saul "went on his way" in verses 3–6. Read Acts 26:13–15 for this account in his own words.
- What did the voice ask Saul? How did the voice identify itself? What instructions were given to Saul?
- Describe the encounter from the perspective of Saul's traveling companions.
- What was the physical result of Saul's encounter with Jesus?
- What did Saul do when he arrived in Damascus?

Interpretation

What a plot twist! The narrative began with Saul of Tarsus, a powerful religious authority marching toward Damascus on a mission to arrest followers of Jesus. It ends with Saul being led helplessly and humbly to Damascus in obedience to Jesus to await further instructions. The passage beautifully closes with Saul blind but truly seeing for the first time, fasting, and waiting on the Lord.

- What does the question "Why are you persecuting me?" reveal about Jesus' relationship with the church? Who did Saul think he was attacking? What was the truth?
- What one pivotal point turned Saul from Jesus' persecutor to his follower? Read 1 Corinthians 9:1, 15:8; Galatians 1:16; Acts 9:27, 22:14, and 26:16.
- Read Galatians 1:11–17. According to verse 15, when did God choose Saul? Who initiates salvation? What was Saul's primary calling? (See Ephesians 2:8–10.)
- Read Matthew 28:19. What were Jesus' final instructions to his disciples, and how was Saul instrumental in carrying out those

GROUP INDUCTIVE STUDY

instructions both before and after conversion? (See Acts 8:1 and 26:16.)

Application

- Saul's identity was shaped and defined by his Jewish ancestry, religious beliefs, education, and accomplishments as a Pharisee. Where do you find your identity? What names, roles, titles, or accomplishments define you?

- Share a time when God allowed you to be physically dependent on him in order to reveal himself more fully to you. How did you respond? What was the result?

- Saul's intense desire to destroy the church was driving him further away from God and deeper into sin. What intense desires and passions seem to control you? How are your desires, passions, or obsessions affecting your relationship with Jesus?

- Have you given up praying for someone to come to salvation because they seem to be a hopeless case? Read 1 Timothy 1:12–17 and reflect on Saul's situation by comparison. Pray as a group for this person's salvation.

- Have you ever thought that your sins were too great for God's grace and forgiveness? Read 1 Timothy 1:13–16. Be encouraged through the life of Saul, given as an example to us, that we can never out-sin God's grace. (See Ephesians 1:7.)

For Further Study

- "God's Sovereignty, Paul's Conversion" by John Piper, www.desiringgod.org/blog/posts/gods-sovereignty-pauls-conversion

WEEK 6

Read Acts 9:10–19

Introduction

God doesn't mind interrupting our lives.

We are unable to improve God's plans for us, and it's unwise of us to try. Jesus interrupted Saul's life in every possible way—from stopping his physical body in the middle of the road to the very intentions and desires of his heart. Finding himself in an unexpected place of dependence, Saul had no idea what to do so he just started talking to God. And God continued that conversation for three days.

Similarly, God interrupted Ananias' life for a calling that seemed frightening and impossible. He was terrified. Nothing about God's request made sense. Ananias had a hard time trusting. He needed to struggle through the evidence stacked up against the call. So Ananias had a conversation with God and emerged in faith that propelled him to action and brotherly love for an enemy.

Is God interrupting your life right now? Perhaps he is calling you in a new direction for his glory, or putting an obstacle in your path of sin. Perhaps he's asking you to take a step that feels risky. Begin, like Saul and Ananias, with talking to God. Heart change happens while we are spending time with our Father. He hears, knows, and will lead us. When we honestly pour out our heart's concerns to him, our Father lovingly displays his character so we can learn to trust him. Then, like Saul and Ananias, we can submit with replenished trust and go forward in the strength of God's power.

Observation

- Paraphrase Saul's story, beginning with his experience on the road to Damascus in Acts 9:1. What new details do we learn about Saul's conversion in Acts 9:10–19? Describe the conversation between Jesus and Ananias.

- What was Saul doing—and not doing—while he waited three days?

- Called out of his murderous path in one miraculous moment, what was Saul's new calling according to 9:15–16?
- What do we learn about Ananias and his faith in verses 10–19? Read Acts 22:12 for more insight into Ananias.
- How does God describe Saul's new identity to Ananias? In what active ways does Ananias' response show that he believes God?

Interpretation

- Read Acts 22:3–5 and 26:9–11. Describe what specific life ambitions Saul had before he met Jesus. How did these change following his conversion? Read Acts 26:16–18, Galatians 1:15–24, and 1 Timothy 1:12–16 and discuss further details of Saul's calling as he describes it.
- What is Ananias' internal conflict about God's command to visit Saul? What prompted these concerns?
- As Ananias and Saul meet, God is bringing brothers together. Read 1 John 4:19–21 and 1 Thessalonians 2:8. Why is it significant that in Acts 9:17, Ananias not only believes who Saul is in the sight of Christ but also in relation to himself?
- Did God need Ananias to go to Saul and lay his hands on him? Why include Ananias in his plan? What can we learn from this as we respond to God's call in our lives?
- Read 2 Corinthians 4:1–12 and 2 Timothy 2:20–21. Consider Ananias and Saul as "chosen instruments" or "jars of clay," both metaphors for being useful in God's work. What does it mean to be a chosen instrument? What can we interpret from Saul's (Paul's) words in these passages?

Application

- How is God interrupting your life right now—i.e., for an immediate ministry that you were not looking for (like Ananias) or to stop you in your sin (like Saul)?

- Talking to God changed Ananias' mind, gave him faith, moved him to action, and gave him unexpected love for someone he previously feared. Do you think of prayer this way? As a believer, when you are fighting your fears or your flesh, how do you struggle to talk things out with God and let him transform you?

- Ananias was not involved in Saul's spiritual progress until the moment God asked him to be obedient to his request. How can you trust God's timing with difficult or bold conversations? What will you do today to emulate Ananias' example?

- God helped Ananias to see Saul in a new light and treat him as a brother. Who in your life has God already given a new identity to, but in your relationship with them, you continue in your fleshly struggle to see them as they were or judge them by their imperfect demonstration of their new identity? What changes need to take place in your relationship? What might God's grace look like in this situation?

WEEK 7

Read Acts 9:19b–31

Introduction

Saul, once a hunter of Christians, was now the hunted.

Following his dramatic conversion on the road to Damascus, Saul not only faced opposition, but the apostles and other Christians didn't believe his experience was authentic. Given his former persecution of the church, it's not surprising that they thought it was a trick. The Jews, appalled by the about-face of their religious hit man, now sought to kill him.

The church is full of unlikely converts. Our Lord is in the business of changing the hearts and lives of those who reject him and persecute his people. God's grace and power, the same power that raised Jesus from death, can change the most hardhearted and unwilling individual. Not one of us is "good enough" to choose God. He alone changes hearts, and we are all in need of his great mercy.

As we study Saul's conversion, reflect on the greatness of our God and his power to save. Saul's story should make us hopeful for those around us who don't know God. Sing God's praise for rescuing us from death and new life in Christ Jesus, because like Saul, without Jesus and his mercy, we too are unlikely converts.

Observation

- How did Saul's conversion immediately affect his actions? How did he demonstrate change to those around him?
- Who plotted to kill Saul when they heard of his conversion? Where did he go to escape?
- Why were the apostles afraid of Saul? Who convinced them of his conversion?
- What effect did Saul's preaching have on the church? How was that manifested within the church?

- What two things were required for the church to multiply? Does the church only grow during a time of peace? Church Father Tertullian (A.D. 160–225) said, "The blood of the martyrs is the seed of the church." How is this true in the context of Acts 8 and 9?

Interpretation

- During his stay in Damascus, Saul "immediately proclaimed Jesus in the synagogues." He was speaking boldly and disputing the Greek-speaking Jews, despite threats against his life. What issues may have been raised in these disputes?

- Read Ephesians 2:1–6. These beautiful words describe how we are saved by grace through faith. What words stand out as evidence of Saul's experience in Acts 9? Why is Saul's conversion so encouraging to believers?

- Christianity is a religion that you enter by conversion. You are not born into it, and it does not discriminate. Read Romans 3:22–26, written by the Apostle Paul much later in his ministry. How do these verses remind you of your need for a Savior?

- In what way does this passage remind us that the gift of preaching is needed for teaching and encouragement in the church?

- When Saul's friends learned that he was in danger, they sent him home to Tarsus. Why did they do this? What is the responsibility of the body of Christ and you as an individual believer to care for another Christian?

Application

Many of us don't have a conversion story like Saul. Some people say they wish they had a more dramatic or interesting story of how they came to know Jesus. Yet we each have a story to share. Every one of us is in need of a Savior, and our sin is deserving of death, yet God being merciful chose to extend his grace to save us. Even if you see your story as boring, you can be encouraged that we have a God who is anything but boring, and the story you have is the one

133

God gave you. He chose you, and he will help you to share the gospel and your story with others.

- Reading about Saul's unlikely conversion compels us to look back to the first time we met Jesus. When you met Jesus, was it a road-to-Damascus experience or something that happened over time? What type of opposition did you face from those around you? How does Saul's story give you hope?

- What doubts do you have about the gospel? How do your doubts make it difficult to share Christ with others?

- When have you been fearful about sharing the good news of Christ? What caused this fear?

- How has the good news of Christ enabled you to live more boldly? Think about a time where you shared your conversion story with others. What compelled you to be bold?

- Think back to a sermon that you've heard recently. How were you encouraged by the preaching?

WEEK 8

Read Acts 9:32–43

Introduction

How many times have we heard the saying "God helps those who help themselves?"

It seems to mean that if we would just get busy, get things done, or turn over a new leaf, God could look favorably upon us. Did you know that saying is not in the Bible? In fact, it is the very opposite of the gospel message!

Consider this story: A man came home from work and declared to his wife that he had become "born again by the Spirit of God." They were not churchgoers; in fact, they had been known to make jokes about "Bible Thumpers." The wife feared he had gone crazy.

Though he was not looking for God, God had come to him by placing him in the time and place to hear and embrace the gospel of Jesus Christ and to be "raised from the dead" spiritually. The man was changed, and it was not his doing. He no longer wanted the party life they had lived. He gave up drinking and drugs. He was reading his Bible and talking to his wife about Jesus. One day she angrily screamed at him, "It feels like you are having an affair with this Jesus!"

As time went on, she began to ponder the amazing changes she witnessed in her husband's character. There was no doubt that something had changed. What she witnessed in her husband was used by God to soften her heart toward Jesus, and within just a few months she too was born again, and their family legacy was forever changed.

This is what we see in Acts 9:32–43 as Jesus, through Peter, heals the paralyzed man and gives Tabitha life again. Aeneas and Tabitha are recipients of God's amazing grace, and Peter is given the incredible privilege of having God work powerfully through him.

In all of these scenarios, the people were completely powerless to change their circumstances or their hearts. But God raised each of them from the dead, physically or spiritually, in order to display his power to heal and restore.

Observation

- Lydda was a town on the Plain of Sharon, between Jerusalem and Joppa on the coast. Why was Peter in this region?
- Find Joppa on a map of ancient Israel (in a Bible or online). Who summoned Peter to Joppa and why?
- Explain what occurred in Lydda.
- In verse 34, who does Peter say is the source of healing?
- What was happening when Peter arrived in Joppa?
- Describe Tabitha and her value to the saints.
- What was Peter's response as he encountered Tabitha?
- What was the result of Peter's actions following his arrival at the Upper Room?

Interpretation

- Read Acts 3:1–7, 9:34, and 40. What consistencies exist in Peter's healing ministry? In each story, to whom is Peter careful to attribute healing?
- Why did Peter immediately direct Aeneas to "rise and make his bed"?
- What do verses 35 and 42 reveal about the purpose and the result of these healings?
- Read John 11:38–45. Compare the response of the people when Jesus raised Lazarus, with the events in Acts 9:32–43.
- What effect did miracles have on evangelism in the early church?

Application

- In what ways have you embraced the erroneous belief that "God helps those that help themselves" by taking credit for a situation getting better or being resolved?

- How have you neglected to give God the glory for the healing and redemptive work he has already accomplished in you?
- Describe a time when you have felt powerless in a situation and yet experienced the presence and power of God in your life. How did this bring about a heart change in you? How has this been used as a testimony of God's power to those around you?
- List some ways God may be leading you to step out in obedience to his call on your life and serve in a way that will bring him glory.

WEEK 9

Read Acts 10:1–48

Introduction

When God speaks, are you swift or slow to respond? Maybe you frequently delay, ensuring you understand before proceeding. Perhaps you immediately rush to fulfill the command, saying "Yes, Sir!"

This is the contrast we see in Acts 10 between Cornelius and Peter. Both are faithful, devout men of God, both receive distinct messages from the Lord, and both immediately identify God as the source of the message. Yet only Cornelius, a Gentile not considered worthy by the Jews, is immediate in his obedience. Peter, a disciple of Jesus, questions God three times before he finally obeys. Why?

Questioning God's direction is not uncommon for Peter. From the first time Peter is called in Luke 5:4–5, throughout his time with Jesus in ministry, and until Jesus' crucifixion, Peter often questioned Jesus before obeying. There are times when even devout Christian leaders hesitate to obey.

In Peter's case, his hesitation may have been because God's vision and message was almost unbelievable. Because of the dietary laws established hundreds of years earlier (see Lev. 11), God's people did not dine with unbelievers; the danger of being exposed to something unclean was too high. With time, restrictions were also applied to their association with the Gentiles. Not only was Gentile food unclean, they were as well. Though Jesus later went on to fulfill the law (Mark 7:1–23; Matt. 15:1–20), thereby nullifying Old Testament ceremonial laws, Jewish opinions about the Gentiles remained largely the same.[14]

In the end, because both Cornelius and Peter were obedient, God's all-along plan of bringing his Son to the nations took a giant leap forward. The Gentiles heard about Jesus, knew him as their Savior from sin, received the

---

[14] Note on Acts 10:13 in *The ESV Study Bible* (Wheaton: Crossway, 2008), 2103.

Holy Spirit, and were baptized publicly. If there was ever a time to be grateful for man's obedience to God, this was it.

Observation

- Describe the character qualities of Cornelius in Acts 10:1–8.
- Describe the character qualities of Peter in Acts 10:9–16.
- Describe the vision that Peter saw in verses 11–13.
- What was Peter's objection to God's command?
- Identify the commands given by God to Cornelius and Peter that required obedience.
- At what point did Peter understand the meaning of the vision God gave him?
- What did Peter do in verses 34–43?
- According to verse 35, who is acceptable to God?
- According to verse 43, who receives forgiveness of sins? How is forgiveness received?
- According to verse 44, what happened while Peter was preaching?

Interpretation

- Read Genesis 12:1–3. Through Abram, who would be blessed?
- Read Matthew 28:19–20. Peter was present for this command from Jesus, and knew that Jesus is part of Abram's lineage. Why was he reluctant to believe that God wanted him to proclaim Jesus to the Gentiles?
- Read Acts 2:1–5. In what way were the disciples fulfilling the command in Matthew 28:19–20?
- Peter states that Cornelius knows it is unlawful for a Jew to associate or visit with someone from another nation (10:28). What does this suggest about the implications of what is about to happen?
- What is Peter getting at when he says God does not show partiality in verse 34?
- What is the significance of Peter's words "just as we have" in 10:47?

- What is the significance of Peter's willingness to stay with the Gentiles for a few more days?
- Describe five ways we see God at work in this passage to bring the Gentiles to him.
- In chapter 11, Peter gave a report to the Jerusalem church about the Gentiles receiving the Holy Spirit. Why was it important that other believers were present for the event in Caesarea in chapter 10?
- Peter said "no" to God before understanding his command. What may have driven Peter's initial response? What prompted his eventual obedience?
- The Jews had many restrictions about associating with Gentiles. What harm might that have caused? Discuss the possible consequences of disobedience if Cornelius and Peter obeyed Jewish law instead of God's command.
- Whose activity is primary in this account? Whose activity is secondary? What is most important about Luke's message in chapter 10?

Application

A lot is happening in this section of Scripture, but we will focus on how we as Christians respond when we are asked by God to obey.

- Describe a time when you didn't immediately obey something God called you to. Why did you hesitate? Describe a time when you immediately obeyed. What caused you to respond to God promptly?
- In John 10:3b–5, Jesus talks about his sheep knowing his voice. When have you heard Jesus' voice? When have you heard the stranger's voice? How do you know the difference?
- Describe ways we image God to others (i.e., believers and unbelievers) in our obedience.
- Showing partiality isn't just about Jew and Gentile. We may also discriminate against someone for other, more superficial reasons (James 2:1–9). How have you subscribed to extra rules or shown

partiality with regard to those with whom you share the gospel? How have you judged others based on your personal legalisms?

- Are you tempted to doubt your salvation or standing with God when you are slow to obey? According to Romans 8:35–39, what separates us from God? According to Acts 10, who empowers our obedience?

WEEK 10

Read Acts 11:1–18

Introduction

Imagine your parents have just introduced a known gangster and drug dealer as your newly adopted brother. This guy, who loved to harass and cheat your family, now has equal standing with you—and didn't even have to shower first! Now it's your job to tell your siblings about the new addition. Will your news be welcomed?

Gentiles, once rejected and unclean by the Law's standards, were now welcomed into the family of God, causing some of the Jewish brothers to object. After all, the Lord had told them, "For you are a people holy to the Lord your God, and the Lord has chosen you to be a people for his treasured possession, out of all the peoples who are on the face of the earth" (Deut. 14:2).

Rome was a self-glorifying people that oppressed Israel. They were tolerant of Israel's worship of the one God as long as it didn't interfere with the worship and obedience to Caesar.

To be sure, the addition of the Gentiles to the family of God was shocking: not only was God reconciling himself to the "unclean," he was reconciling two groups of people divided by hostility.[15] Peter was now faced with the difficult task of defending the new brothers to the Jews.

Observation

- Why did Peter go to Jerusalem?
- Who criticized Peter and why?
- How did Peter respond? What additional information do we learn from this passage compared with the same story in Acts 10?
- What question does he end with, and what is the response?

---

[15] Darrell L. Bock, *Acts* (Grand Rapids: Baker, 2007), 42–43.

Interpretation

God had changed Peter's own heart from repulsion to acceptance. He described how God moved to bring about this controversial change through the preaching of the gospel and then the ultimate proof: the gift and indwelling of the Holy Spirit that mirrored Pentecost. It meant that Jesus, the Jewish Messiah, would extend salvation to everyone, even a Gentile. It is not the Jewish cultural and ritual identity that legitimizes spiritual standing before God. Only through Jesus' perfection alone can anyone be deemed clean.

- Was Peter easily convinced to accept the Gentiles?
- Why is it significant that the Gentiles received the Holy Spirit the same way the Jews did at Pentecost?
- After Paul finished his story, a hush fell on the crowd. This was a point of decision for the Jewish listeners. Would they "stand in the way" of God's plan and reject the Gentiles, or accept what the Spirit was doing and continue to follow Jesus? Why was the Jewish followers' approval important?
- Read Romans 11:1–24. God uses the metaphor of his people being an olive tree. Gentiles are the wild olive shoots that have been grafted in. God has been cultivating his "olive tree" nation born through Abraham, and now because of their rejection of his salvation through Jesus, the whole world is offered his salvation. With whom is God severe? To whom is he kind? Why?

Application

"For I am not ashamed of the gospel, for it is the power of God for salvation to everyone who believes, to the Jew first and also to the Greek" (Rom. 1:16). It is hard for some of the Christian Jews to accept that anyone who believes could be acceptable to God without becoming Jewish first. But the Holy Spirit is at work, and they respond by worshiping God, their Father. All have sinned and are unclean, both Jew and Gentile (Rom. 3:23). We cannot make ourselves clean. Jesus is the only one who lived a perfect life and died in our place to pay for our sin. John says, "If we confess our sins, he is faithful and just to forgive us our sins and to cleanse us from all unrighteousness" (1 John 1:8–9). He has made a way for us all to be clean in God's eyes.

- How are you "standing in the way" of what God is doing? Why? What change does this account inspire in you?
- How has God's sovereign plan gone differently from what you expected, and how have you responded?
- Are your past sins causing you to see yourself as unclean or dirty? What lies have you believed? What truth will you now believe?
- From what do you gain your worth, identity, or righteousness instead of Jesus? Do you expect more from people than God?

WEEK 11

Read Acts 11:19–30

Introduction

If you are a "Christian," know that this derisive, mocking nickname for the followers of Jesus Christ was first coined in Antioch.

Antioch, the Syrian city three hundred miles north of Jerusalem, was the home of a new and growing church. Planted by followers of the Way after they were scattered to the ends of the earth following Stephen's martyrdom, this young church plant blended Jewish and Gentile believers and united them in their love for Jesus. Antioch's Christians knew that living by faith in a community of believers went hand in hand with sharing the gospel with their neighbors. So great was their growth that the Jerusalem church sent a helper to support them. Church planters have to stick together!

The church at Antioch is an example for us today of a church plant that grew in influence and service to others. Because the hand of the Lord was with them, from its humble beginnings, people were saved, trained, and sent out. Saul, their first lead pastor resident, taught a great many people. By God's grace, their faithfulness allowed them to bless others in need and the church was founded to the glory of God. We can learn much from our fellow Christians at Antioch by observing how they responded to God's blessing.

Observation

- Read the passage carefully. If you are not familiar with the story of Stephen and the persecution that followed, it can be found in Acts 6:1–8:3.
- Read verses 19–21. What did the believers who were scattered and persecuted do? What was the result? To whom is the result attributed?
- How did the church respond in verse 22?
- What did Barnabas and Saul do for the church in verses 23–26?

- What are the three things, in order, that Barnabas did in verse 23? What was the result?
- Who was Agabus (vv. 27–28)? What did he do? What was the response of the disciples (vv. 29–30)?

Interpretation

Interpretation of God's Word can often become entirely too subjective if we do not rely on the Holy Spirit to interpret Scripture through itself. Take a moment to pray and ask the Holy Spirit to open your heart and mind to what he has to share with you today from his Word.

- In verse 23, what did Barnabas see? Read Acts 4:33, 15:11, 18:27, 20:24, 32, and Romans 12:3 for more evidence of this.
- Read the following verses that include the phrase "hand of the Lord" as it is used in Acts 11:21. What is the meaning of the phrase based on these verses: Ezra 7:8–10, 8:18; Nehemiah 2:8, and 18? What can we learn about the character of God based on God's movement as recorded in these verses?
- Read the following verses for more insight into Barnabas' character: Acts 4:36–37; 9:26–28; 13:1–2, 43–51; 14:1–3, 13–15, 21–28; 15:1–3, 12, 25–26, 35–36, 39–40; and Galatians 2:13. Describe his character from these verses. What qualified him to go to Antioch? What role might someone with similar gifts play in the church today?
- The spiritual gift of prophecy is demonstrated by Agabus in this passage. Read 1 Corinthians 14. What distinctions are made between the gifts of prophecy and tongues? In what way are these gifts to be exercised? Read 1 John 4:1–3 and Hebrews 4:12. How can we determine if a prophecy is from God?
- Read 1 Peter 5:5–6. How do you see the characters in this passage living this out well?

Application

- In verses 19–21, no one in particular was named the leader(s) of the group that was preaching the gospel, yet "a great number . . . turned to the Lord." How does this encourage you as you share your faith with others?

- In verses 22–26, Barnabas enters the scene. How did he respond to what was happening in the church in Antioch? After reading about his character, how are you challenged by his example? How will you strive to better emulate him?

- This passage marks a huge change in the church at the time. Greek-speaking non-Jews heard the gospel and responded in belief and repentance. It was unnamed believers who cross-culturally shared the gospel with these Hellenists. How have you allowed cultural or ethnic differences to deter you from sharing the good news of Jesus with others?

- When Agabus prophesies about the coming famine, the church responds by sending financial support to the affected areas. How do you give sacrificially to support those in need? Is this giving joyful?

- In verses 20–21, the work of spreading the gospel is twofold: the Word is preached, and the Lord's hand is on it so that belief results. Which do you tend to rely more heavily on in witnessing to others: your own ability to share the gospel skillfully or the Holy Spirit's movement in the hearts of the hearers? While we should all rely completely on the Holy Spirit to inspire our words and give us discernment when sharing the Good News, we should also prayerfully prepare for such moments. Pray today that God will help you to do both well by his grace.

APPENDIX FOR LEADERS

How to Use the Daily Devotions

The following devotions were written in the hope that families would rally around the Word of God, grow in relationship together, and discover how the Holy Spirit fills believers, empowering them to proclaim the good news of Jesus to family, friends, and neighbors.

Every day, you and your family are provided with a short passage from the book of Acts to read and discuss. A series of questions and illustrations will help you dig deeper into the passage and apply its message to your lives. Each devotion is capped off with a suggested prayer.

Don't feel bound to follow every step, read each word, discuss all the questions, or pray every prayer. Follow the Holy Spirit's lead and allow the conversation to progress as you see fit.

Also, don't stress if you miss a night or get off track with your conversation. Family time can often be a little chaotic, and things come up. Just be prepared to pick up where you left off. Most families aren't able to do devotions every night of the week, so each Scripture portion is divided into five devotions for five days of the week, allowing you the freedom to figure out what weekly rhythms make sense for you.

Finally, while the book of Acts is certainly religious history, it's also much more. Remember, God's people still have the same Holy Spirit enabling them to live with passion and partner with him to see lives changed by Jesus. That same Holy Spirit will help you and your family be bold in your witness of Jesus to one another, your church, and all those whom God has placed in your life.

How to Use the Small Group Study

This study has been designed to help your small group discover the power of the Holy Spirit that enables his people to provide witness to the greatness of Jesus Christ. We all need the presence of a community to encourage us when inevitable opposition to the gospel arises, and also to spur one another on to good works (Heb. 10:24).

Each study begins with an introduction that serves as a springboard for conversation in your group. There's no need to read the introduction verbatim, if that feels stodgy. Just familiarize yourself with the content beforehand and give an overview of the Scripture passage, linking it with timely examples or testimonies of what God is up to in your own community.

After setting the stage for the week's Scripture reading, questions are provided so that the group can dive into application. Use these as a way to stir up conversation. Some questions are simply opportunities to share testimonies, while others are offered as challenges for growth. Take some time beforehand to jot down notes of what questions are best suited for your specific group, and see where the Holy Spirit leads the conversation.

Last is a suggested prayer. It's common to leave little time for prayer, but be encouraged to provide a good amount of time for this. From prayers of praise to requests for help with life's common struggles, to petitions for healing and everything in between, we need to be refreshed by God's presence and strength. Pray with expectation that God will do great things in your community. He is a loving Father who loves to give good gifts to his children.

How to Use the Inductive Group Study
What is an inductive study?

"Inductive study" refers to a particular type of analysis that uses the Bible as the primary tool for learning about God and receiving instruction about how to live a godly life. Our goals for this type of study are to observe the text, interpret its message as we listen to the Holy Spirit, and apply its meaning to our lives.

The steps are simple. Begin by reading the "Background and Introduction" of the assigned Scripture. Then, read the associated passage, and pray about what it is communicating, asking God to open your hearts and minds so that you can learn more about him.

Next, examine the passage in light of the context in which it was written, with an eye toward the whole of Scripture. Then, zero in on the words on the page. Good questions to ask as you study include *who, what, where, when, why*, and *how*. Here are some examples of how you might use these kinds of questions:

- Who was the writer's original audience?
- What issue was being addressed? What was being said?
- Where and when did this take place?
- Why was the message given?
- How was the message communicated?

Other helpful questions are listed under the "Observation" heading.

The "Interpretation" will come from the text that is before us, as guided by the Holy Spirit, who opens our eyes and reveals what we need to see. Again, please pray that God will be guiding your mind as you examine the text. Keep in mind that as we study Acts, it's important to follow the text and let it define the context and audience before jumping into our own life application. That's where the above-mentioned questions are so helpful: Who comprised the early church as recorded in Acts? What struggles and hardships did they face? What facet of the Good News is highlighted in Acts, and why? The historical account in Acts is an exciting time in the early church. But remember, the Holy Spirit who was at work in the early church is the same Holy Spirit at work in the church today. How is the Spirit empowering the ministry you've been called to?

Next, don't miss the "Application" questions. In the fourth section of the weekly study, questions that focus on practice are provided: How does each verse shed light into your life? In what ways does the Scripture show you your need for Jesus? What is your plan for change going forward?

Finally, pay attention to how God is stirring and convicting your heart. It's here at this intersection where we apply the Word to our lives. We become more like Christ, and our relationship with God is deepened.